Rules of
Engagement

The Shocking Marriage Series

Jerry McColgin

ISBN 978-1-64191-731-5 (paperback)
ISBN 978-1-64191-732-2 (digital)

Christian Faith Publishing, Inc.
832 Park Avenue
Meadville, PA 16335
www.christianfaithpublishing.com

Printed in the United States of America

Contents

This book is dedicated to my parents, who in their seventy plus years together showed me what it was like to truly have a shocking marriage.

Preface

I am an engineer by training and have spent the bulk of my professional life developing new products and making processes more efficient. I began my career doing time-studies in a washing machine factory then worked my way up in corporate life to the point of running major global projects. After that, I started and ran my own consulting business focused on strategy and innovation. My customers were typically large companies that made consumer products. Many of these products were once leaders in the market but over time have become tired and lost their uniqueness. The service that I provided was to figure out why these products were no longer relevant and to suggest changes that would put them back on top again. To accomplish this, I spent time with the consumers who used the products and uncovered the unmet, sometimes unspoken, needs that they had. With that understanding in hand, I would help companies to either modify their existing products or develop brand-new products that could satisfy the needs of their target market.

On a personal note, I love marriage and I love being married. It grieves me when I see people just going through the motions or simply cohabitating with their spouse. My wife, Tara, and I have created and conducted workshops with churches and with small groups in an effort to improve marriages. It hadn't occurred to me until recently that our approach to creating better marriages is really no different than my efforts in resuscitating tired products. While human emotions and relationships are infinitely more complex than manufactured "things," there are still many similarities. Analyze and understand the current state of the product (relationship), gain a deep understanding of the customer's (spouse's) unmet needs, and develop enhancements (guidelines) that will rejuvenate the product (marriage). After doing this on a volunteer basis for several years, I felt led to take this on in a more focused manner. I became ordained as a Christian minister and now find myself seeking to assist and enhance marriages on a regular basis.

Our marriage is not perfect; no marriage is. But our track record is strong. As of the writing of this book, we have completed our thirty-fifth year of marriage. I can honestly say that in many ways, thirty-five was been the best year yet. We both come from long lines of successful marriages. At the time of my mother's death, my parents had been married for seventy-three years! Likewise, when Tara's dad passed away, her parents had been married for fifty-six. I have three older brothers who collectively share over 140 years of marriage. There has been no divorce in either of our lineages as far back as we can see. I don't tell you this to boast or to imply that we are special in any way. But just as a master carpenter has learned tips and tricks to making beautiful furniture, there are behaviors and attitudes that we can share to help you enhance your own marriage.

We are surrounded by a world of broken marriages. Our culture has veered far away from God's plan for marriage, and many couples have abandoned their dreams of what marriage could be and instead settle for simply hanging on. My hope is that you'll apply the principles from this book to create a marriage that is based in God's original design. A relationship meant to *joyfully* last until "death do us part."

This book will focus on key areas of marriage using life-tested philosophies, tips, and techniques to help you proactively create and grow the type of relationship that you really desire. These aren't merely relationship theories, but rather actual processes that can be adopted by any married couple who is willing to commit to long-term growth and success.

As you read this book, discuss it with your spouse and complete the exercises at the end of each chapter. Through these discussions, you'll discover some attitudes and behaviors in your relationship that may be counterproductive, but you'll also learn some positive new actions that can make your marriage stronger and more enjoyable.

Your spouse should be your greatest relationship here on earth, and you should want nothing more than to share your life with them. It's not hard to be married, but it takes effort to have a *shocking marriage* that positively stands out from our culture.

If you're going through this as a small group study, refer to the Study Guide at the end of the book. There you will find questions and discussion starters that are appropriate in a group setting. My hope is that by studying this with other couples, you will learn that you are not alone in the issues or challenges that you face in your own marriage. That will allow you to encourage one another both now and in the future.

1

Shocking Marriage

We live in a culture that puts far more emphasis on weddings than it does on marriages. In 2016, the average cost of a wedding in the United States was $26,645 and took fourteen months of planning. That's an average! That means that for every simple wedding you've been to, there is at least one extravagant one to offset it.

Another study shows, that in that same year, only 44 percent of engaged couples entered into any form of premarital counseling. Of those that did, the median time spent in counseling was around eight hours.

Think about it this way. As a culture, we spend fourteen months planning for a single eight-hour day. But we only spend one eight-hour day planning for a lifetime of marriage! Is it any wonder that our divorce rate is so high? Many marriages start off on a high note and slowly erode over time. Once the honeymoon phase is over, comfort sets in. Comfort is soon followed by complacency, then boredom, and finally discontent. It is in this phase where marriages dissolve or, due to family responsibilities or convenience, continue in a dead and loveless condition.

Marriage has become fodder for humor both on television and in the movies. Couples are routinely seen disparaging one another or sneaking around trying to conceal their activities from their spouses. We find ourselves so deeply immersed in this culture that we have accepted, and sometimes even adopted, these negative attitudes and behaviors The God-ordained sanctity of marriage has degraded over time, and the stigma once associated with divorce has all but vanished.

These negative attitudes and behaviors have become so common that we are somewhat shocked when we see a long-married couple still truly in love. Be honest. If you see a couple in their forties or over who are enjoying conversation, flirting, holding hands, or engaging in playful banter, you probably assume they are newlyweds or on their second or third marriage. We're just not used to seeing couples act like that after an extended time together.

A shocking marriage stands apart from these cultural norms. Regardless of the size or cost of the wedding, the early stages of marriage are just a baseline in terms of happiness and satisfaction. Through focus and intentionality, the marriage builds. There are still challenges and tough seasons, but a shocking marriage gets better with time.

This book is targeted at couples who are ready to commit to a better marriage. A shocking marriage. That does not imply that your marriage is currently in trouble, nor does it insinuate that your marriage is mediocre. It's simply recognizing that no matter where you are in your relationship, there's room for improvement. If you're in a good marriage, think in terms of great. If you're in a great marriage, work toward making it extraordinary. If you're engaged to be married—perfect! No better time to plan for a promising future than now. The days of settling for a marriage that is just okay are over. It's time to dream big about what your marriage could and should be.

This book will guide you through marriage reflection, analysis, and planning that will enable you to grow your relationship to new levels that you may not have considered possible. It will provide you with opportunities to create marriage guidelines to ensure that you and your spouse are working toward the same short-term goals and long-term vision.

Casting a Vision

Envisioning your desired future is the first step in the process. Over the course of my professional career, I've launched several new project teams, organizations, and even businesses. Some were overwhelming successes, and others, quite frankly, were outright failures. In almost every case, the difference between success and failure was the quality of the vision at the outset. Those efforts with a bold, solid vision were far more successful than those where I attempted to direct the future as I went along.

In business, a vision should be lofty and cause an organization to stretch in order to achieve it. Amazon didn't strive to be just a seller of books. Their vision statement is "to be Earth's most customer-centric company, where customers can find and discover anything they might want to buy online." Twitter didn't dream of becoming another texting replacement app. Their vision is "to give everyone the power to create and share ideas and information instantly, without barriers." These companies have bold visions to be the biggest and the best at what they do.

Likewise, a solid vision for marriage should be something that causes both spouses to look to the future, inspiring them to work together to achieve something meaningful. When revisited over time, this vision should allow a couple to make any necessary adjustments to ensure they headed in the right direction.

No engaged couple dreams about entering into a dull, routine relationship that both partners find merely tolerable. Rather, they dream of a lifetime of love and family and growing old together. Unfortunately, that is not a vision but rather an overplayed stereotype. Relationships change over time, hopefully for the better but, unfortunately, sometimes it's for the worse. No couple that's been married for ten years will claim that their feelings for each other haven't changed over time. Without ongoing and intentional effort, when the honeymoon phase begins to fade, the simplistic dream fades right along with it. Working toward a shared vision will keep the marriage on track and growing in a positive direction.

So ask yourself: What do I want my marriage to look like five years from now and beyond? What would it take to create a shocking marriage?

Elements of a Vision

If you've ever worked in a corporate or a nonprofit setting you may have participated in a meeting where you worked on creating a vision statement. Oftentimes these are long tedious meetings that devolve into endless wordsmithing. Memories of this experience may scare you away from exerting such an effort for your marriage. Don't make it that hard; just capture some thoughts or goals that you can both agree to work toward. You're not carving anything permanently into stone. These can and should be revisited and revised as needed over time. In fact, that would be a very positive activity to do as a couple every few years.

Here are some elements that are included in the marriage vision I created with my wife, Tara.

- We want our marriage to honor Christ in all that we say and do.

- We want to raise a healthy and happy family but keep the spousal relationship a top priority.

- We want to *love being married* to each other and will take efforts to make that so.

- Fun is a top priority for both of us.

- We will assess our relationship periodically and focus on areas where we can make improvements.

Remember, a marital vision is not a day-to-day set of rules that must be followed. It is a compass to keep you headed in the right general direction. The key is to recognize when you start to go off course and make the necessary adjustments to get back on track.

Use the questions at the end of the chapter to help capture your thoughts. Write them down and create a starting point. Your vision can and should be revisited over time and will be perfected as you grow together as a couple.

Remarriage

Maybe this is not your first marriage. You've been married and divorced and find yourself either preparing for or in another marriage now. Like so many others in your same situation, you bring battle scars in to your current relationship that you gathered in your past. Even though your past marriage failed, that does not mean that you as an individual are a failure. God has a plan for you and your life that includes your current spouse.

The people I know who are on their second (or third or even fourth) marriage seem to fall into one of two camps. The first camp wants more than anything to blot their first marriage from their memory. They see it as an awful experience and choose to never spend time thinking about it. The last thing they want is to discuss that relationship with their new spouse. While it may seem like a way to avoid stress, that attitude does nothing to change behaviors. In time, their old habits and behaviors return and create the same problems they encountered before. As a result, they find themselves once again in an unhappy, unhealthy marriage, and threat of another divorce hangs over their heads.

The second camp I see is very different. These people also went through a failed marriage, but instead of ignoring their past, they spend time analyzing it. Instead of trying to place blame, they look at their own attitudes and behaviors and determine what they could/ should have done differently. They talk openly with their new spouses about these issues and ask to be held accountable to the changes they desire to make. They typically make a commitment to one another that they never want to go through another divorce and agree that they are both in the relationship for the long haul. They have learned from the past and commit to working together toward a better future.

I have seen that those who openly consider their past and choose to learn from it tend to be in much more satisfying relationships than those who attempt to block it from their memory or refuse to take a critical look at what actually went wrong. Learn from the Spanish philosopher George Santayana: "Those who do not learn history are doomed to repeat it." Don't fall into the same patterns and traps that you did the first time around.

Creating a Shocking Marriage

Shocking marriages don't just happen. The first and key step to creating a shocking marriage is intentionality. Making a conscious effort to focus on your marriage by prioritizing your spouse and their needs will set you apart from the masses. It doesn't mean ignoring other key people in your life. It just means not taking your spouse for granted and assuming that you can tend to them later.

A friend told me about her dad's experience in coaching a girl's middle school softball team. He agreed to do this as a favor to his daughter, and he saw it as an opportunity to spend time with his two granddaughters on the team. His experience with this was less than ideal. It turned out that the team was in a fairly affluent area, and many of the girls on the team were also on other, sometimes more prestigious, softball teams. As a result, he never knew how many kids would actually show up for practice or even for a given game. There were a few times when they didn't have enough players to field a team. This team was not a top priority for many of these girls, so they came when they could but missed out otherwise—often without even bothering to notify the coach. Being on this team was just another item on an overcommitted list. There was virtually no chance that they could have been successful.

Too many marriages in our culture resemble the dynamics of this team. Spouses become just another person on the list who needs to be attended to. Sadly, because they are taken for granted, they fall to the bottom of the priority list behind kids' needs, career needs, social needs, church needs, and other distractions. It's no wonder that over time, these marriages dissolve. Just like the softball team, they have no chance of winning.

You may no longer be a newlywed. In fact, you may have been married for years or even decades by now. You may not be on your first or even your second marriage. *Where you have been is of far less importance than where you are headed.* God does not want you to be in a mediocre marriage. He wants you to be blessed abundantly in this regard. If you want to pursue and achieve a shocking marriage, there's no better time to start than the present.

In 2013, contemporary Christian artist Casting Crowns launched a song called "Thrive." I love the chorus. It includes the following:

> We know we were made for so much more Than ordinary lives It's time for us to more than just survive We were made to thrive

I can't think of a better descriptor for a shocking marriage. As you read through this book, I want to challenge you to consider areas of your marriage where you may be just surviving. Be honest with yourself. These areas may not look any worse to you than what you see in most other marriages around you. But that's not what we're shooting for. We're looking for excellence in marriage. We're looking to thrive. We want the world to look at our marriages and find them shocking.

What does a shocking marriage look like? I liken this to the way that Supreme Court Justice Potter Stewart described his threshold test for obscenity in 1964: "I know it when I see it." Let me give you examples of shocking marriages in couples that I've seen or I know personally:

- The couple in their nineties that hold hands while sitting in church every week.

- The couple married for thirty-plus years that playfully flirt together in the checkout line at the grocery.

- The couple that prioritize date nights and leave their kids home with a sitter.

- The middle-aged couple in a cooking class together for the first time.

- The couple that speaks highly of each other when alone with their friends.

- The spouse that avoids correcting or criticizing their partner as they recount a story to friends.

- The couple that has a "secret rendezvous" midweek during lunch.

It's not that any one of these activities is shocking but, rather, the intentionality that lies behind them. Couples that do these things work at marriage and are always seeking to head to a better place. They don't take each other for granted. They give their partners high priority as they go through life. They avoid complacency. They realize that their spouse is a gift from God who should be honored.

Discussion Questions

What are the vision elements that you would like to strive for from this day forward? It all starts with a conversation. Work through the following questions with your spouse:

- Independently list five words that you would use to describe your ideal marriage relationship (e.g., fun, passionate, stable, comfortable, etc.). Once you have each listed your words, share your list with your spouse. What words do you have in common? What words are different? Are you surprised at any of their words? Discuss this as a couple.

- What long-term marital goals (vision elements) do you and your spouse share?

- How well is your current relationship heading toward those goals? What needs to change if a course correction is needed?

- Think of couples who you believe have great (shocking) marriages. What are the specific things about them that make you think that? What specific things have you seen them do to indicate that they give each other priority?

- What is one "shocking" behavior you can incorporate into your marriage in the next week? The next month? The next year?

2

Build A Solid Foundation

Anyone who listens to my teaching and follows it is wise, like a person who builds a house on solid rock. Though the rain comes in torrents and the floodwaters rise and the winds beat against that house, it won't collapse because it is built on bedrock. But anyone who hears my teaching and doesn't obey it is foolish, like a person who builds a house on sand. When the rains and floods come and the winds beat against that house, it will collapse with a mighty crash.

—Matthew 7:24–27

Marriage is a beautiful and tangible application of this teaching. Marriages built on the rock of Jesus will weather the inevitable storms that come in life. Those built only on passion or feelings are like the house built on sand. Living on the beach sounds great at the outset. Who doesn't want a life filled with white sand, crystal-blue water, and palm trees? But living in a cabana isn't so appealing when a storm comes. When the wind and rain of hardship starts to tear at the structure of your marriage and there is nowhere to go for refuge from the storm, the beach loses its luster. If you don't create a foundation built on rock, your marriage may not survive. Marital collapse doesn't happen all at once. Just like a house, a relationship built on a shaky foundation degrades over time. You may attempt repairs, but without shoring up the foundation, these fixes will be mainly cosmetic and short-lived.

We all know couples whose relationship is built on sand. At first, they seem to have it all together in terms of family and careers. But as time goes on, we begin to notice the cracks and missing shingles that exist within their marriage. They attempt to conceal the most visible issues for awhile, but over time, they simply quit bothering with repairs. At some point, they decide that the effort required to rebuild the relationship is just too great. At that point, they cut their losses and walk away from the whole thing.

Contrast this with the couple that builds on a solid foundation. Notice here that I say *couple*. If only one partner is striving for this, and the other is not willing or interested, the foundation will still not be solid. The issues they face in their marriage may be no different in terms of frequency or severity, but because of their sure foundation, they are able to weather the storms that come in life. They know the value of maintaining and repairing their relationship, which allows their marriage to appreciate over time.

Our Story

My wife, Tara, and I got married at a young age. I was twenty-one and she was a few months short of her twenty-first birthday. We began dating in high school and continued doing so into college. Like many young couples, we were passionately in love and didn't want to put off being together. Due to our conservative upbringing, neither of us considered it okay to move in together out of wedlock. We got married before my senior year (her junior year) and moved into married student housing at Purdue University. At that age, creating a vision or building a foundation on rock was the last thing on our mind. We just wanted to be together, get through school, find employment, and ultimately transition to our "adult lives." Selfishly, our focus was on what was best for each us as individuals. I went to my classes, and she went to hers. Little or no attention went into planning what would be best for us as a couple. We simply assumed we would figure life out as it came.

The first ten months of marriage went by smoothly and quickly. Being in the honeymoon phase of marriage, conflict was rare and short-lived. Our frustrations were little different from our nonmarried friends, mostly centered on school assignments and class projects. The first real test in our relationship occurred as my senior year came to a close. Though I had an engineering degree from a great school, I graduated in the midst of a nasty recession. I went to every interview on campus and applied to as many openings by mail as I possibly could but heard back from none of them.

Graduation was exciting, but the feeling of accomplishment was short-lived. The lease on our campus apartment expired within days of the ceremony. With no job in hand and no home to live in, we found ourselves as a newlywed couple moving back home with my parents.

I was blessed with great parents, but moving back into their home as a young married man was humiliating. I'll never forget the look in Tara's eyes as we moved our few possessions into their home, "What have you gotten me into?" they asked. She had a full year left before graduation, didn't know what her future would hold, and wondered if she would be able to finish college. To add insult to injury, she was being moved in to live with her in-laws. I felt both helpless and useless. I had a wife whom I could neither support nor begin a serious adult life with. There were several quiet days spent worrying and wondering.

Time passed at a snail's pace, but after a couple of weeks, I got a call from one of the companies that I had applied to by mail while still on campus—Whirlpool Corporation. They had an opening for an entry-level industrial engineer at their washing machine factory in Clyde, Ohio. I jumped at this opportunity and within days found myself driving the five hours to the interview. Things went well, and within a couple more weeks (of incredibly anxious waiting), I got a job offer. Within a month, we found ourselves moving to Ohio to finally begin our adult, married life.

Things got exciting again. I threw myself into work, and Tara began taking classes at the University of Toledo. New beginnings, independence, and adulthood were now underway. The very things that we had been waiting for now became the primary focus of our lives. We had new friendships, personal endeavors and work/class schedules to fill our time, and we took our relationship with each other for granted. We were building our marriage on sand, and we saw no reason to do anything differently.

Our life in Ohio continued on. The honeymoon phase of marriage was wearing off, but things were still okay. We found ourselves assimilating into our new community. I was an engineer at a huge factory in a small town, and Tara drove an hour each day to attend classes. Being new in my job, I wanted to fit in and establish relationships. Most of my coworkers were native to the area, and many of them had worked their way up from the factory floor. I don't know if it was unique to this particular small town or simply the culture of factory life, but I found myself being exposed to influences and values that were foreign to me. As an example, most people I worked with were married, but many saw no real problem with "fooling around on the side."

Gossip was rampant in terms of who was sleeping with whom. A typical Friday afternoon would include a trip to the bar across the street for happy hour, where many of my coworkers wouldn't go home until the wee hours the following morning. As this was contrary to how I'd been raised, I was surprised by their attitudes and behaviors. I remember asking one respected guy in our department, "How does your wife put up with you staying out all hours and carousing with women?" His response was simply, "She's got five kids, where's she going to go?" While his answer repulsed me, he was an ongoing, unhealthy influence that I worked with every day. Though I didn't agree with many of the attitudes around me, my immersion in this culture began to rub off on me. The language I picked up and the lack of respect I began showing Tara all began to increase. Since everyone else went to happy hour on Friday, I found myself going as well. At first, it was just a drop-in visit, but over time, I found myself staying far longer than I'd promised Tara. When I did get home, I was typically not in a state of mind to be very focused on her needs. She began to resent my lack of respect, my drinking and my absence from home.

In an effort to establish relationships outside of work, we got involved with various community-based organizations (in hindsight, it seemed like everything except church!) where we met a variety of people and made new friends. One night we went out with two other couples. One of the couples was each on their second marriage. We had just finished dinner at their home when they began to argue about something that (apparently) had occurred earlier in the day. While this was uncomfortable for the other four of us, it was a situation we had witnessed in the past. The argument escalated quickly, and before we knew it, the wife was storming out of the room screaming at her husband, "I should just divorce you. I left my first husband for far less." In hindsight, I'm not sure if we were more shocked by the magnitude of her threat or by the casual manner in which her husband dismissed it, as if it were nothing. While he was somewhat embarrassed this happened in front of us, his response was simply to smile and wave his hand. "She'll get over it."

When Tara and I got home that night, we were both shaken by what we'd experienced. We sat silently on the couch for quite a while. The evening's events forced us to contemplate our own marriage. Finally, with a tear in my eye, I looked at Tara and asked her, "Is divorce something you would ever threaten me with?" It took her much longer to respond than I would have hoped. The conversation that ensued cut me to the core. I didn't realize how much my newly acquired selfish behavior had affected and even injured her. Truth be told, at some level, she had begun to question our future together, deeply concerned at the negative direction we were heading. While I was seemingly oblivious, she had begun to see our "house" for what it was—a degrading structure with no solid foundation.

As our conversation went on, I apologized for my behaviors and told her that I never wanted to consider divorce. She responded that was not her desire, either, but went on to say that things needed to change for that to be off the table. Once I was aware of the issues with our relationship, I could no longer ignore them. Being an engineer by training, I began to work on the problems that had surfaced one by one. It was exhausting, but I put in the effort, and Tara could see I was trying. After a couple of weeks, I nervously approached her and said, "I never want to get a divorce. I promise I will stay with you forever if you'll have me." Her response back was the most comforting I'd ever heard. "I agree. I'll never threaten divorce or leave you either."

It was during that period that we came to realize that our relationship was not as stable as we had perceived it to be. We didn't yet know what it meant to build our marriage on the rock of Jesus, but we knew that we did not want to remain in the condition we were in. It was time to move forward.

Soon after this, I was promoted to a new job in Michigan. Tara and I both saw this as a chance for a new beginning where we could start building our marriage in a more positive manner. Our first child was turning three, and I felt strongly that we needed to find and start going to a church somewhere. I had gone to church every Sunday as a kid, and I was determined that my children would do the same. While Sunday mornings were never my favorite time growing up, I still figured it was the right thing to do for them.

Our goal was to find a church that would be comfortable for both of us. By comfortable, I mean a place where we could attend on Sundays but not be expected to do much else. A place where we could make good friends, but not ones who were too pious or judgmental. If we could walk away after service feeling good about ourselves and inspired to be better people in the upcoming week, that would be a plus.

We found an Evangelical Free Church near our home. While we had never heard of this type of church, in our minds it sounded perfect. In the age of sugar-free, caffeine-free, and fat-free, we assumed this would be a church that was free of evangelism. The last thing we wanted was to be pressured in our faith or trying to recruit other people to join the church.

It turns out we were wrong. Quite wrong. It turns out that this was a Bible-believing church that had a tremendous focus on outreach. That first Sunday found me squirming in my seat as the sermon convicted me of my lifestyle and made me aware that there was something (someone) missing from my life. In spite of our discomfort, the people there were warm and loving, and we felt ourselves drawn back there in the following weeks. Within a few months of attending, we both accepted Jesus into our lives as our Lord and Savior. God began directing us individually and reshaping us as a couple. It became clear that we needed to build our marriage on a new foundation that is Jesus Christ. That has remained our focus ever since.

The Trinity's Role in Marriage

The theology of the Trinity is foundational to the Christian faith and also foundational to marriage. While we may not understand everything about the Trinity, the basic idea is that God exists in three parts: God the Father, Jesus the Son, and the Holy Spirit. That's one God. Three in one. As you will see in the following, each part of God has a role in our ongoing relationships.

God the Architect

We see in the very first verses of the Bible (Genesis 1) that God created everything, including the sun, the planets, earth, water, animals, people, even life at a microscopic level with complexity beyond our comprehension. We also learn from scripture that God is all-knowing (omniscient), all-powerful (omnipotent), and everywhere at every time (omnipresent). This clearly puts God in the role of Master Designer or Universal Architect, the ultimate creator and designer of life as we know it.

As with other aspects of His master design, marriage originated with God and is mentioned in the second chapter of the first book of the Bible (Genesis 2). God declared that it was not good for man to live alone, so He created a helpmate for Adam. In verse 25, we see that Eve is referred to as Adam's wife. They became one flesh and were intended to stay together for eternity. But as the story continues, sin entered the world, and the first couple was exiled from paradise. All forms of trouble and distress entered the world including, we can assume, problems in marriage.

As fallen people, our culture has veered far away from God's original plan. This is not a recent phenomenon. We see early on in the Old Testament examples of infidelity and polygamy. King David so lusted after the beautiful Bathsheba that he had her husband assigned to the front lines of battle, knowing that he would be killed. His son, Solomon, the wisest human who ever lived, had eight hundred wives and over two hundred concubines! All of his earthly wisdom could not ultimately overcome the influence these women had over him. As time went on, Solomon began building temples to the various gods that his wives worshipped, and he ultimately fell out of favor with God.

Ecclesiastes 1:9 (ironically written by Solomon) says, "What has been will be again, what has been done will be done again; there is nothing new under the sun." Thousands of years later, many couples abandon God's plan and decide to do things their own way. They look at the architect of the universe and everything in it and say, "I understand your intention, but I think I know a better way . . ." The results speak for themselves. Marriage is destined to work better when we build our relationship according to the Master Architect's design.

Jesus the Foundation

As we saw in Matthew, building your foundation on rock happens by hearing Jesus's words and following His teaching. Jesus is the foundation on which we should build our marriages. What does that mean? What does that look like?

Before you can build your marriage on Jesus as your foundation, you must first have a *personal* relationship with Him. You have to see your need for Him. Romans 3:23 says, "*For all have sinned and fall short of the glory of God.*" There's nothing you can do on your own power that will make you worthy of being with God. No amount of community service, good works, spirituality, or church attendance will earn you eternal life. But God didn't leave you in a hopeless state.

John 3:16 says, *"For God so loved the world that He gave His one and only Son, that whoever believes in Him shall not perish, but have eternal life."* Salvation is a free gift offered to everyone. All you have to do is admit you can't get there on your own and accept the gift that is provided through Jesus. As believers, we cherish grace and view it as the most remarkable gift that could possibly be received.

As humans, we are naturally wired to desire justice. Justice is defined loosely as getting something that is deserved. Right should be rewarded and wrong punished. Fortunately, scripture shows us that we are not limited to receiving only that which we deserve. Jesus died on the cross that we might be forgiven for the wrongs we have done—past, present, and future. It is only through His sacrifice that we can be seen as blameless and considered worthy of eternal life.

That is where grace comes into play. Grace is defined as the undeserved favor of God for those who are otherwise under condemnation. If we truly got what we deserved, none of us would be worthy to enter heaven to spend eternity with God.

Just as we are freely given grace from God, we are called to extend grace to others. That holds especially true for our spouses. How do we do this? We do this when we incorporate kind words and encouragement into our language. We do this when we don't condemn or attack our spouse. We do this when we forgive. We do this when we don't hold on to past issues. And we do this when we show love even when we're not especially feeling it. It is not reasonable to be able to show grace if you've not experienced it. Understanding and accepting God's grace is a critical first step to putting Him first in your marriage.

If you and your spouse have accepted Christ, that's a great starting point. Now you need to agree to make Him the foundation of your marriage. Jesus should be the primary relationship for each of you as individuals. After Him, your relationship with each other comes second. If you get this out of order, your foundation is not solid, and your marriage will suffer. You cannot put your faith on a back burner and expect to receive God's blessings, assistance, or direction. Make Jesus the focal point of your entire relationship.

Holy Spirit—the Source of Power and Security

So you've committed to God's design for your marriage, and you've decided to build your foundation on your collective faith in Jesus. What else is needed? Homes work better when they are connected to a power source. Electricity, natural gas, and even Internet are no longer considered luxuries, but rather basic needs. You might be able to survive in a home without these things, but life is certainly easier when they are provided.

I have a Nest thermostat in my home. It is a "smart home" device that learns my preferences and behaviors over time and adjusts the temperature accordingly. It knows when we're home and when we're away. While we used to constantly be tweaking the old thermostat, we now always feel comfortable in our home while at the same time saving money by not overheating or cooling an empty house. As a result, I have ceded control over to this device. It has learned my preferences and my dislikes. I now trust that it knows best and always has me in an optimum setting.

I have a friend who got an identical Nest thermostat as a present. It's been several months, but he has not gotten around to installing it yet. It sits in a box on his counter. Just like me, he owns a Nest. His Nest has as much capability as mine does, but he has chosen not to enjoy any of the benefits that it offers. I've talked to him about how easy it is to use; in fact, I've even offered to install it for him. However, he likes to be in control and doesn't like the thought of this smart device running his environment for him.

Marriages are no different. You can have a well-designed relationship built on a foundation of faith, but it will require a tremendous amount of effort on your part if you try to sustain it without wisdom and power from the Holy Spirit.

In John 14:26, Jesus says, "But the Advocate, the Holy Spirit, whom the Father will send in my name, will teach you all things and will remind you of everything I have said to you." Jesus promised the Spirit to all who believe. While all believers have access to the Holy Spirit, many choose not to engage with Him. As Christ's followers, all we have to do is open up and begin to consciously interact with the Spirit in our lives. He's available, powerful and desires to have a relationship with each one of us. When we allow the Spirit to power our lives and our marriages, life becomes much simpler. Galatians 5:22–23 says, "But the Holy Spirit produces this kind of fruit in our lives: love, joy, peace, patience, kindness, goodness, faithfulness, gentleness, and self-control." What marriage wouldn't be better if it exhibited these characteristics?

In a "smart marriage," the Holy Spirit provides more than power. He also provides protection and security for those who choose to be connected. Just as you might have smoke alarms and carbon monoxide detectors in your home to warn you of unseen dangers, the Spirit can do the same for you in your marriage. Every marriage will have natural seasons of highs and lows. During low seasons, negative thoughts may creep into your mind regarding your spouse. Hints of dissatisfaction, mistrust, or even unjustified anger could be examples. It's at these times that you need to seek the guidance of the Holy Spirit to check the source of these thoughts. Remember, there are forces that don't want believers to be in happy marriages. Ephesians 6:12 tells us, *"For our struggle is not against flesh and blood, but against the rulers, against the authorities, against the powers of this dark world and against the spiritual forces of evil in the heavenly realms."* The Spirit will help you to recognize these thoughts for what they are—destructive input intended to cause discontent in a relationship. Once you see this, you can literally pray them away.

God wants us to have blessed marriages that bring Him glory. It grieves Him when He sees married believers sin against each other through conflict, separation, and divorce. And it certainly damages the credibility of the church when our marriages are no different from those in our culture. But we can't have the marriage that God intends for us to have if we don't make Him the center of it. When we try to bolster and protect our marriages with our own efforts, we're no different than the world around us.

Questions

- What does the author mean when he talks about having a marriage built on rock instead of sand?

- What would you say that your marriage is currently built on?

- Are there ways that you could "shore up" your foundation?

- Using the house analogy, what areas of your marriage should you focus on maintaining? What areas, if any, need immediate repair?

- Have you prioritized Jesus as being *first* in your marriage? What does that look like?

- Are you utilizing the power the Holy Spirit provides in your relationship, or are you doing things on your own strength? How could you begin to plug in to the power that God has provided for you?

3

Rules of Engagement

I know a guy who manages his investment portfolio on a near daily basis. He wants to see what stocks are overperforming and which are falling short. He has a series of formulas and guidelines that he uses to direct his buying and selling. Based on his findings, he makes continuous adjustments in an effort to maximize his return. He once gave me this investment advice: "You've got to keep a constant eye on this thing or it will get away from you. It's critical to spot trends— see how the market is reacting to various stimuli. By making little adjustments on a regular basis, you can avoid any huge surprises." To this day, he takes tremendous pride in his savvy investment strategy.

He's divorced now. It's not because he spent so much time managing his money, but rather that he spent way too little time watching his marriage. It turns out his wife had been unhappy for quite some time. He hadn't noticed. She craved attention and affection from him that she wasn't receiving. He hadn't noticed it. Over time, she grew further and further from him emotionally. Eventually, she was lured away by the attention of another man who was willing to satisfy her needs. That he noticed!

When his wife left him, he was shocked and felt completely betrayed. He was unable to grasp the role he had played in the failure of his marriage. He didn't realize that had he spent a fraction of the time on the relationship with his wife that he did on his finances, he could have seen trends coming, established some guidelines, and made adjustments. He may have been able to save his marriage. As it turned out, the return on his marriage investment bombed.

As I said in the previous chapter, shocking marriages don't just happen, they are intentional. It takes determination and discipline to create and maintain a great marriage. Unfortunately, this kind of self-discipline does not come easily. This is not a new condition, nor is it tied directly to our current culture. Nearly two thousand years ago, the apostle Paul wrote about this very issue. He says this in Romans, "I don't really understand myself, for I want to do what is right, but I don't do it. Instead, I do what I hate" (Rom 7:15, NLT). He elaborates a couple of verses later, "And I know that nothing good lives in me, that is, in my sinful nature. I want to do what is right, but I can't. I want to do what is good, but I don't. I don't want to do what is wrong, but I do it anyway" (Romans 7:18–20). I've got to wonder how many marriage counselors have heard these same sentiments?

It's important to note that God Himself first envisioned the concept of marriage. He didn't intend for us to enter into such a complex relationship without Him. If we rely on our own strength in marriage, we will most certainly fall short of His expectations, as well as our own. The good news is, as believers, we can partner with God in our marriages. Ecclesiastes 4:9–12 provides a great picture for what this should look like.

> Two are better than one,
> because they have a good return for their labor:
> If either of them falls down,
> one can help the other up.
> But pity anyone who falls
> and has no one to help them up.
> Also, if two lie down together, they will keep warm.
> But how can one keep warm alone?
> Though one may be overpowered,
> two can defend themselves.
> A cord of three strands is not quickly broken.

You and your spouse are more capable and powerful together than either of you could possibly be on your own, especially when you are committed to the same vision and goals for your marriage. Add the Holy Spirit as the third strand, and your cord (relationship) is not easily broken. It's ultimately about being Spirit-disciplined, not self-disciplined.

Creating our Rules

Once Tara and I determined that we would build our future relationship on rock instead of sand, we realized that we would need to do things differently moving forward. We decided that we would focus on two different areas. First, we would intentionally take the time to periodically do a self-assessment on our relationship. This simply consists of having a reflective conversation. How have things been going? What's gone well? Where have we struggled? Where are we headed? The goal of this was to ensure that neither of us was assuming how the other was feeling in terms of the marriage. Knowing that we always go out for a nice dinner on our anniversary, we agreed that could be a great time to have this discussion. Having it on a set and memorable day has kept us from procrastinating or forgetting about it all together!

Having the annual assessment was a great step, but we realized that we had a need to try to improve things on an ongoing basis as well. One of the areas where we struggled surrounded conflict, an area where our individual styles were radically different. Our arguments, though infrequent, caused so much frustration for each of us that we knew we needed to do something different. Never fighting again seemed unrealistic, so in a time of peace and calm, we created some guidelines on which we could both agree. The goal was to ensure conflict would ultimately move our relationship forward and not cause lasting damage. That discussion created the foundation of something we came to call our marital rules of engagement (ROE). The *Cambridge Dictionary* defines "rules of engagements" (ROE) as: "orders that soldiers fighting in a war are given about what they can and cannot do." It's not that we saw ourselves as combatants in our marriage, but we liked the parallel.

Implementing rules of engagement surrounding conflict improved our relationship immediately and dramatically. Once a spat was over, it was over. No more walking around the house not speaking. No more cold shoulders in bed, and no more fear of starting the argument over by saying the wrong thing. Over time, this worked so effectively, we realized we could apply it to other areas of our relationship. Sure, fighting fair is critical, but how many other areas would benefit from having preestablished guidelines? What about intimacy? Raising children? Maintaining external relationships? Making financial decisions? Marriage is so much easier when you go through it with agreed-upon guidelines that you have created together.

Rules will be as unique as the couples that create them. No two personalities are identical, nor are any two marriages. Tara and I love nothing more than spontaneity. We have friends who think we are crazy the way that we turn on a dime or run off and do something on the spur of the moment. Ironically, that's one of our proactive rules.

Rule of Engagement: Keep the marriage interesting— never stop surprising.

That particular rule might not fit your personality at all. You might be a person who hates surprises. The thought of not thoroughly planning an event might make you cringe. That's okay! Our rules are for us, and your rules need to suit you. The key is to create guidelines that you both agree will be good for your relationship and that you both agree to follow.

As we've grown and changed as a couple, our rules of engagement have grown with us. This is not a document that you file away but rather a living document that changes as your life and your relationship naturally evolves.

Some couples have their rules of engagement in a printed form that they revisit and edit on a regular basis. Some rules are stricken, some added, and some simply modified. That's beautiful. Other couples treat their rules of engagement more as a guideline they discuss and agree upon in a much less formal setting. That's great too. The most important thing is to get past the assumption stage, have an honest conversation, and agree on a path forward together. Ultimately, it's about the relationship, not about the rules.

However you want to create and maintain your rules, you must have accountability. That could mean pulling out the official list and pointing to a rule that has been violated. It could be a verbal reminder that "we agreed we would..." Your list is of minimal value if you can't both agree to honor it and to hold each other accountable. It can be hard to be called out on a rule in the midst of a heated discussion. But remembering that each rule was created for the overall long-term good of the marriage can help you to pause, take a deep breath, and honor your commitment.

Biblical Rules of Engagement

God has laid out in His Word a plan for marriage and relationships, and we can create rules of engagement for our marriages that honor and follow His patterns. There are some rules that should be shared by all Christian couples. Examples of these are as follows:

- We will remain faithful to each other (Exodus 20:14).

- We will strive to honor God in all aspects of our marriage (1 Corinthians 10:31).

- We will honor and respect one another, considering our spouse's needs first (Romans 12:10).

- Divorce is not an option. It will not be threatened or considered (Malachi 2:16, Matthew 19:9).

This is not an exhaustive list but rather a reminder that scripture provides us with a great model to be followed. As you grow in your faith, allow God's word to continue to speak to you in terms of how best to operate within your marriage.

Types of Rules

Marriage rules of engagement generally fall into two categories: situational rules and proactive rules. Situational rules determine how you behave in a given, known situation. These rules might govern how you will engage in an argument or how will you act in situations that are a part of your regular routine (e.g., I will always kiss my wife before I leave the house, I will call my husband every day when I am traveling). These are not intended to be punitive but rather exist to encourage behaviors that you have both agreed will enhance your marriage.

Vice President Mike Pence has talked about rules that exist within his marriage. He would not dine with a woman unless his wife was present. He also would not go to a party where alcohol was served unless she was with him. These rules fly in the face of our current culture. In fact, the media had a heyday on this topic, calling him misogynistic and biased against women because of these. But they are situational rules that work for Mike and Karen Pence. You could say they have a shocking marriage!

You can probably think of several situations that you and your spouse regularly face. Determine which of these you would benefit from by having a situational rule. In addition, be aware of situations that might not immediately come to mind where you could also benefit. If you find that every time you leave your in-law's house you get into an argument, this might be an opportunity for a rule. What behavior while there could change that would avoid the oncoming conflict? Look for negative patterns in your marriage that you would like to change. What situations cause conflict? What situations lead to other problems? Your goal should be to eliminate those areas that cause repeated issues. It's not about stifling the argument. It's about adapting the behavior to eliminate the need to argue.

The second type of rules are proactive rules. These transcend a given situation and are more aligned with heading toward your established vision. They may be harder to quantify, but their goal is to make your marriage better over time. These rules are very personal, and they emphasize emotions as much as they do to actions. As an example, "I will provide a safe environment for my wife and family" has associated actions but is ultimately measured by the wife's feeling of security. Likewise, "I will strive to keep fun in our marriage" could deal as much with style of conversation as it does with physical activities. These rules will evolve over the course of marriage, and that is okay. We change over time, so does our relationship, and so should our rules. Have rules in place that make sense for the season you are in, which you both agree move you closer to your vision.

I remember a specific evening when Tara and I went with our family to dinner at a local restaurant. We were sitting around a big table laughing and talking and enjoying the fellowship as well as the food. As I looked over Tara's shoulder, I noticed a couple come in and sit in a nearby booth. I had never seen this couple before, nor did I know anything about them. But I watched them come in, sit down, look at their menus, and order food without ever saying a word to each other. After they ordered, they both began fiddling with their phones. Their food came, and they ate in silence. I didn't sense any hostility between them; instead, there was an air of boredom surrounding them. This grieved me. Based on their age, my guess is they were empty nesters that had nothing to talk about now that the kids were gone. While I continued to enjoy my meal and laugh with my family, I kept watching to see if anything changed at their table. They may have exchanged five or six words by the end of their meal, but they were finished and paying their bill as we were still enjoying ours.

If the behaviors of this couple were extremely rare or isolated, I probably would not have given it much thought. But watching them reminded me of so many couples that I know. I realized that Tara and I would one day be empty nesters as well. This sparked a conversation when we got home. I told Tara about the couple and how sad their lack of interaction seemed. I expressed my hope that our marriage would not succumb to boredom and routine. She agreed with me and suggested that we make a new proactive rule.

Rule of Engagement : Strive to keep life together work talking about.

Admittedly, there are a lot of facets to a rule like this, but it encourages each of us to do interesting things both together and individually. We always converse at dinner and never allow our phones to take priority. To this day, if I come to the dinner table in a rough mood or find myself distracted with other issues, she will call me out on it. When Tara does, that couple immediately comes to my mind, and I find myself starting to talk about something. It may feel forced at first, but within no time, we're in the midst of an interesting conversation.

Summary

Rules of engagement are a simple tool that you can implement within your marriage. It's something that you create together with the goal of continuously improving your relationship. Over time, some rules will change, and others will be added. Periodically revisiting your rules will ensure that you are both adhering to them, and it will also provide you with an opportunity to create new rules that are pertinent to your current situation.

Start simple. Create a few rules and see how they work. Determine if you are growing closer to your shared vision for your marriage or if you are drifting away from it. If you do find yourselves drifting, discuss the behaviors that are causing your challenges and create new rules to turn that trend around.

Discussion Questions

1. Where is God in terms of your marriage relationship? What steps could you take to give Him priority?

2. Do you see the value in creating rules of engagement within your marriage? What concerns might you have? Is this concept something you can both get behind? Discuss any benefits or concerns that you might see as a couple.

3. Are there situations in your marriage that you repeatedly face that might benefit from situational rules of engagement? What are they (be specific)? What might those rules look like?

4. What are some broader areas that you want to focus on in your marriage (think fun, security, stability, passion, etc.)? What proactive rules could you create to help you in this area?

4

Dealing with Conflict

Some people make cutting remarks but
the words of the wise are healing.

—Proverbs 12:18 (NLT)

It is impossible for two people to live their lives together and always
share the same opinion. While in some situations having these differ-
ing points of view is acceptable, there are other times when you need
to align your views in order to move forward. Sounds easy, doesn't it?
If we could only keep it at a nonemotional level, it would be. But the
reality is we are emotional beings, and most of us struggle with pride.
As a result, when we find ourselves in a dispute, we spend our time
trying to develop persuasive arguments to justify our point and bolster our defenses. We are convinced that if our spouse just *understood*
what we were trying to say, any argument would simply go away. We
have an unrealistic expectation that goes something like this.

Once you *hear and understand* my point, you will quickly realize the error in your thinking. With this newfound understanding
in place, you will fall silent as you immediately begin to reflect and
plan a new life path based on your sincere and enlightened change of
heart. You will thank me for illuminating you in your area of darkness, and our relationship will move forward in a manner far better
than before. If by some chance you don't react as I expect, it must

be because you clearly didn't *hear and understand* my point. To show my commitment to our relationship, I will state my point again, only this time with more volume to better facilitate your hearing. In addition, I will offer you more specific examples to help you see the flaws in your perspective. I may have to repeat this process multiple times, but I am willing to do so and remain convinced that in time, you will come around. How's that working for you?

If you fundamentally agree that you are both on the same team, and headed toward a common goal, it makes it infinitely easier to get through times of conflict. While you may think you should do something your way, they clearly think you should do it their way. So who is right, and who is wrong? Though that is where our thinking starts, it is actually an irrelevant question. The reality is both approaches are probably viable. So now what? In these times, we have to honestly ask ourselves a key question: Is it more important that you get to your defined long-term goal (vision), or is it more important that you prove yourself right in this near-term situation?

Is It Possible to *Win* an Argument?

Consider the following scenario. You find yourself in an argument with your husband. You clearly see things from different perspectives, and each of you believes that your opinion/solution is correct. After what seems like an eternity of animated discussion, he throws up his hands and says, "You are right. We'll do it your way." That may be the answer you hoped for, but it isn't being expressed with the correct amount of appreciation and sincerity. You suspect he doesn't really agree with you, and that further increases your anger. Instead of seeing this as a now-resolved issue, you express your disbelief in his concession, and that leads to further fighting. Your original intent was to convince him to agree with you, but at this point, you are mad because he claims that he does.

You have officially found yourselves in a no-win situation. You start out wanting to win at all costs, but even if your opponent concedes, you aren't satisfied. Nothing can be said that will end this dispute on a positive note. No matter what you agree to do, it won't feel right. To make things worse, both of you will probably begin to avoid this topic in the future because of the frustration or pain that you experienced during the argument. Whatever the issue was, it hasn't gone away, and it certainly hasn't been resolved.

Disagreements may be inevitable in a marriage, but they needn't be ugly. While your natural tendency may be to try to change the attitudes or behaviors of your spouse, the better place to start is with yourself. Ask yourself the following question: Is my goal to work through a given issue and arrive at a better place, or is it to simply prove myself right and my spouse wrong? Proverbs 13:10 says, "Pride leads to conflict; those who take advice are wise." Pride is a major source of conflict in many areas of life, no less so in a marriage. When your spouse confronts you with an issue, your first prideful reaction is to rebut the confrontation and defend yourself. From there, an argument erupts, as neither party wants to back down from their original stance. When pride is on the line, there can be no winner. Both sides will ultimately feel defeated. In a shocking marriage, individuals learn to check personal pride at the door and instead learn to take pride in their relationship. This shift of mind-set can do wonders in preventing unnecessary conflict in your marriage.

Once you've learned to put your pride aside, disagreements are no longer based on who is right and who is wrong. Both partners can see a situation from very different perspectives, each of which has value. Time and energy once spent trying to win your spouse over to your side can be now be used to gain understanding. It's possible that elements of both perspectives could be incorporated into the outcome. When this happens, you will find yourself in a better place than had you somehow won the argument. Realistically, it could even be done at a lower decibel level in a shorter amount of time. Imagine walking away from a heated discussion feeling great about the direction you are heading together? It's possible when humility allows you to listen and work together to get to a better place.

Pride can also prevent forgiveness. If you feel you have been wronged, hearing your spouse apologize and express remorse is not enough. Pride keeps a record of wrongs, a mental scoreboard tracking who has wronged whom and to what degree. As the list increases on both sides, it clearly becomes harder and harder to get back to zero.

Jesus provides the example of how we should treat our spouse with forgiveness and humility. Does Jesus hold a grudge when we sin against Him? No. Does Jesus withhold forgiveness when we commit the same sin over and over? No. Does Jesus stop loving us when we put our needs first and act without considering Him? Still no. We are all called to become more Christlike in our lives, which extends to our marriages. Matthew 18:21–22 says: "Then Peter came to Jesus and asked, 'Lord, how many times shall I forgive my brother or sister who sins against me? Up to seven times?' Jesus answered, 'I tell you, not seven times, but seventy-seven times'." As you develop a heart and attitude of humility and forgiveness, you will find that many arguments can be avoided altogether.

Our goal should not be to learn how to avoid arguments, but rather to learn to respect each other's perspectives and opinions. Again, it is critical that you have collectively agreed upon a common vision and foundation for this to be possible. But with these in place, you can learn to take conflict and turn it into a blessing.

Conflict Is Inevitable

"As iron sharpens iron, so one person sharpens another" (Proverbs 27:17). Friction and conflict within any meaningful relationship is inevitable. Just as the verse in Proverbs suggests, it is the violent inter-action between two pieces of iron that causes the sharpening. When this happens, sparks fly, small particles are removed from each surface and newly honed, more effective surfaces result.

I once had a boss tell me, "If you and I agree on everything, I have no need for you whatsoever." There was much wisdom in that, but hearing a perspective that is different from our own can sometimes be difficult, especially if this falls into an area that we feel strongly about. It takes effort to hear such a message with an open mind and to give it proper consideration. Our prideful nature starts with the assumption that if I have a strong opinion on something, then I am inherently right. If your opinion differs from mine, you are fundamentally wrong.

How do we overcome this natural tendency? For us, it became a foundational rule of engagement.

Rule of Engagement: We will exert our energy in building up our relationship, not in tearing it down.

Sounds pretty basic, right? It is. But basic is not necessarily easy. It starts with increasing our personal self-awareness. You have to ask yourself very honestly what is the motivation behind the point you are trying to make? Are you trying to improve the marriage, or are you seeking personal gain at the expense of your spouse? When the focus is on building the relationship, many arguments can be avoided altogether.

Sometimes you can derail an argument before it really gains steam, perhaps in a humorous manner. Let me give you an example.

I came home one time after a two-week international business trip. While I was thrilled to see Tara and the kids, I was jet-lagged and admittedly grumpy. More than anything, I just wanted a peaceful family dinner with some casual conversation. Tara, on the other hand, had been dealing with both of our sons for two weeks with no help whatsoever from me. From her perspective, she was looking forward to getting a break by having me reenter the family and resume parenting duties. We sat down to eat together and began talking about our time apart. It was great to be reunited, but the reality is we both had considerable frustration just under the surface. As we were eating, the boys started misbehaving and fighting with one another. It really grated on my nerves in my exhausted state. I scolded them several times, but their behavior only continued to get worse. Tara seemed oblivious to their actions, which frustrated me further. Finally, out of sheer desperation, I looked at Tara and said, "Would you please do something?" She looked at me, her eyes got big, and she calmly replied, "Okay. I will." At that point, she flicked the spoonful of mashed potatoes she was about to eat directly into my face.

I don't know who was more shocked, the boys or me. But they both burst into outrageous laughter. I looked at each of them in turn then said, "Oh yeah? How about this?" I then flung a spoonful of food at each of them. At that point, it was game on and turned into a full-blown food fight right there in our kitchen. It took a while to clean up the mess, but a situation that was turning ugly suddenly became a memory that our boys fondly recall twenty years later. Tara's unexpected reaction broke the negative momentum and changed all of our perspectives for the better.

Differing Styles

Like most couples, Tara and I came into our marriage from very different family cultures. This was not something that we ever openly discussed, so we never considered the implications of our upbringing on our relationship. In many instances, the cultures in which we were raised were in direct conflict. One of the earliest examples of this to emerge was in the manner and style in which we argued. Growing up in my household, there were disagreements and differences of opinion between various members of the family, but I seldom, if ever, heard raised voices or shouting. Conversations would get intense and very focused but would eventually end in some form of agreement with all parties (at least on the surface) satisfied. This scenario would occur fairly often. Since that is how I was raised, I assumed this to be both normal and commonplace.

I brought this set of beliefs and behaviors into our marriage. When something bothered me, I would communicate the issue as soon as possible. The mere act of getting it off of my chest would make me feel better and allow me to move on. My hope would always be that we could work through the issue and find some form of resolution, but if not, I could still move past it once I'd vented. If Tara chose not to respond, that implied (in my mind) that she was in agreement. From my perspective, we didn't argue very often.

When growing up, Tara's family handled conflict in a completely different manner. Open confrontation was not the norm. When someone was angered or offended, the acceptable response would be to go off on their own and internalize the issue in hopes it would simply go away over time. Sometimes it would in fact go away, but many times, it would result in the silent treatment near term, or even in physical ailments longer term. Stomach ulcers and other stress-induced conditions were common across her family. Just as I had done, Tara assumed what she experienced to be the way of all families.

When you bring two such different cultures together with no advance planning, fireworks are sure to occur. Getting things off my chest made me feel better, but it had the opposite effect on Tara. She was more like a pressure cooker. My complaints or criticisms would essentially turn the heat up on her feelings. My words would bother her, but she would suppress her feelings and not say anything at the moment. To a simple guy like me, no reaction meant no problem, but that was far from the truth. The thing about a pressure cooker is when the relief valve blows, all the pressure that's been building up comes spewing out. That was Tara.

Imagine my surprise when from my perspective, I would do or say something seemingly minor, only to watch her go ballistic. Once she blew, I would hear about every infraction and offense that I had committed since our last argument. "And another thing" became the most dreaded words I would hear from her. Arguments escalated quickly. I would find myself matching her anger and intensity out of some primal sense of self-defense. It was not uncommon that after these outbursts, we would each be so frustrated and angry that we would storm out of the room and not speak about it (or anything else) for a few days.

After one nasty argument, Tara got so overwhelmed that she grabbed her keys and her coat and left the house. As I heard the garage door closing behind her, I panicked. She had just driven off, leaving me at home with our kids. Where was she going? When would she come back? Would she come back? I tried to call, but she didn't answer. The worst possible thoughts ran through my mind, and I had no idea what to do. When the inevitable "where's mom?" question came from the kids, I nearly broke down. Several hours later, she came back in the house. She walked right past me but told our son that she had "needed some alone time" and simply gone to see a movie. While I was relieved she was back, I was now furious that she had left me in that manner. Anger bred actions that bred more anger. It was a dangerous cycle.

Our arguments began to run together. It got to the point where Tara's breaking point became less and less. What we didn't realize in our youthful years of marriage is that an argument not effectively resolved is an argument still occurring. One day, in between spats, we agreed to sit together and talk about the situation that was quickly becoming unbearable. We agreed to take turns talking and to respectfully hear each other out. We spoke of what made us angry and how we felt when disrespected by the other. It is important to note here that we did this in a time of nonconflict. It is not realistic to think that a conversation of this nature could take place in the heat of battle. In what I now realize was a moment of God-inspired wisdom, we started to make a list of specific actions that made each of us crazy. We talked about these items and explained the details and feelings behind them. We asked questions of each other to make sure we had a clear understanding of each concern. But most importantly, we revisited the fundamental agreement that we had previously put in place. We were both in our marriage for the long haul; divorce was out of the question and off of the table. With that in hand, we both realized that while we would still argue, we knew that we would work to find a way to make up and resolve things. That was huge.

Rules of Engagement for Arguments

Most marital conflicts take the form of verbal arguments. While we may not be throwing physical punches at our spouse, our choice of words can cause lasting damage. It is in our fallen nature to strike back when we are injured. If your words hurt me, my base instinct is to one-up you with an even more critical attack. You've probably experienced the angst of being in an argument like this, one that continues to escalate until one partner breaks or walks away. In time, apologies may be made, but the scars from harsh words inevitably remain. Creating rules of engagement that are specific to conflict can minimize the lasting effect of unkind words.

Our rules of engagement became an agreement, but much more importantly a mind-set that we both agreed to abide by in future disputes. Creating this list took considerable time and effort and has continued to evolve over the years. At first, it required each of us to learn and implement new behaviors. While not easy at first, over time, these behaviors have become second nature to us.

Rules are meaningless if they are not enforceable. In our case, we agreed that even in the midst of a heated discussion, either of us can call a foul if someone crosses a preestablished line. Because we are both committed to this agreement, calling foul causes us to pause, take a deep breath, and acknowledge the infraction. Oftentimes, this is accompanied by an apology, which confirms our mutual commitment to these rules. Just taking this pause in the midst of an argument can reset our emotions. Far too often, as things escalate, cruel words are spoken. This approach stops the argument temporarily before it can run offtrack. It took commitment and discipline at first, but over time it became a habit. Thirty plus years later, we still argue, but we continue to abide by these rules.

The following is a portion of the rules we created for dealing with conflict. These were created for us and our unique personalities and relationship. Feel free to use any of these as they are, or use them as a starting point as you go through this effort with your spouse:

Rule of Engagement: Divorce is not an option and will never be used as a threat.

This was our first rule of engagement and became the cornerstone for all future rules. It reminds us that we are ultimately on the same side. While arguments still occur, we know that we both want the best for our relationship, and conflict that is properly resolved should lead to a stronger relationship.

Rule of Engagement: If something is really troubling one of us, we need to either let it go or bring it up as soon as possible.

Sometimes, given a little time, certain frustrations will just go away. There's more angst created by bringing up some small issues than just letting them dissolve. But you must truly let it go. If after a short period of time the issue is still bothering you, then it needs to be brought up. A given conflict was now focused on a timely, specific issue and no longer a laundry list of past frustrations.

Rule of Engagement: Eliminate absolutes from our language.

Certain words and phrases escalate an argument, while others tend to subdue it. We agreed to drop words like *always* and *never* (e.g., "You never pick up your socks…" or "You always leave the garage door open…"). Nothing puts a person more on the defensive than hearing words like "You never…" or "You always…" As soon as these accusations are made, our mind immediately goes to an exception where that was not the case, destroying the credibility of the accuser and intensifying the argument.

As an example, when Tara told me, "You always leave your socks on the floor," my mind immediately recalled the recent night when I took them off and put them in the clothes hamper. Because of my memory, I believed her accusation was unfounded. Therefore, I had the right and the responsibility to set her straight. In spite of my strong evidence proving her wrong, the argument was far from over. She had a legitimate complaint that my socks ended up on the floor far too frequently. My anger didn't stem from defending my slovenliness but rather from the word *always*. As we talked this through, we agreed that I should pick up my socks and that she had the right to become frustrated when I failed to do so. We both felt somewhat ridiculous at the energy we had put into an argument when we realized we were on the same side.

Rule of Engagement: Use less you words and more I words.

If I am accused of something, my natural initial instinct is one of denial. But if Tara tells me that my actions cause her to feel a certain way, I feel compelled to listen. Think of this one in conjunction with the previous rule. Shift the statement from "You never pick up your socks" to "I get frustrated when I have to pick up your socks so often." This is a simple yet powerful rule. When I'm accused, I get defensive. If I learn that my actions are hurting or frustrating Tara, I am prompted to change my behavior.

Rule of Engagement: Focus on the problem and not the person.

Pointing out the frustration caused by my socks constantly being on the floor is legitimate. Calling me a slob transcends the problem and becomes a personal attack. Just like in a courtroom, words may be stricken from the record, but they can't be unheard. There's no place for belittling or name-calling in a spousal dispute. That will never lead you to a better place.

Rule of Engagement: Know and look to the heart of each other.

Many arguments begin with a misunderstanding. It could be that something was misstated or misheard. If I've said something that hurts Tara, I want her to first consider my motivation and my nature. Is my heart one that would intentionally wound her with my words? If it is not, I hope to get the benefit of the doubt or at least be given the opportunity to explain myself.

Rule of Engagement: Don't go to bed mad, but allow time for resolution.

Ephesians 4:26 (NLT) says: "And don't sin by letting anger control you. Don't let the sun go down while you are still angry." When we first created this rule, it simply stated "Don't go to bed mad." I wanted to resolve every conflict immediately, then kiss and make up. But the rule didn't account for our personalities and the different ways in which we process information. While I can turn on a dime and change my mind, Tara needs to be able to walk away and absorb what has been discussed. We added "allow time for resolution" to help us respect each other's needs. I have confidence when she walks away from an argument that we will eventually come to a resolution, and she feels the freedom to take the time she needs to process before coming to a conclusion.

Know What You're Arguing About

There are many times we find ourselves in a dispute without really understanding the core issue. Having rules of engagement can help to prevent or even rectify these situations. Here's an example of how conflict might occur in a relationship without rules of engagement.

John is an executive at an insurance company. He has been on a two-hour phone meeting with his boss who lives in another city. The boss is frustrated with the overall performance of the company but has been taking much of this out on John. From John's perspective, he has been berated and criticized for almost every decision and action that he's made for the last quarter. When he finally gets off the phone, he feels like he's been run through the wringer, can't do anything right, and may never live up to his boss's expectations. John just wants to get home and leave his frustration at the office.

John's wife, Sue, has been home with her two teenage kids for the day. She feels like she has spent her entire day nagging the kids to get the chores done. The fact that it is late afternoon and many of these items remain undone leads her to feel disrespected and unappreciated. It seems nobody listens to her, and she is at the end of her rope. As she begrudgingly gives in and starts a load of her daughter's laundry, John walks in the back door. She verbalizes the first thought that comes into her head, "Did you remember to go by the store and get the trash bags like I asked you?" she asks John.

Boom!

I need not go into the details of this argument. My guess is that you can create a mental picture of the next ten or fifteen minutes of their "discussion" on your own. Let me help you ramp it up in your imagination. Within moments of the conflict's beginning, Sue says to John, "You never do what I ask you to." She's essentially poured gas on that fire. John yells back, "Nothing I do is ever good enough for you." Here's the point. John and Sue find themselves in a nasty, heated argument within moments of coming together. Over what? Trash bags!

Had John and Sue established their own rules of engagement prior to this, either one of them could have called a foul to assess what they were actually arguing about. After a cooling-off period (just a few minutes), Sue could express that she could get the trash bags later when she runs to the store. John could apologize for forgetting and begin to tell her about the nightmarish conversation with his boss that distracted him. Sue begins to empathize and apologizes for jumping on him. She could then go on to tell John about the frustrations she had been dealing with teen defiance all day. Now instead of heading off into separate rooms no longer speaking, they might just decide to sneak off without the kids and have a drink together where they could further unload their respective frustrations and come to laugh together at the situation they averted. And while they're out, they could grab trash bags!

It is critically important to establish guidelines for conflict during a time of peace. Learn which conflicts are worth working through and which have no real value. If there is benefit to your differences of opinion, you can learn to get both sides expressed effectively and reach a mutual agreement. When there's nothing to be gained in an argument, recognize this early and save the emotional energy for something more proactive.

Keeping the Right Perspective

There is a difference between averting conflict and avoiding it. As hard as you might try to keep an argument from happening, sometimes it's simply unavoidable. The key is to learn to fight fair and not do any lasting damage with your words or actions. Dealing with conflict is really about maintaining a long-term perspective. Knowing that you, as a couple, are both completely committed to the relationship allows you to get through the tough days. Even in the midst of a nasty argument, you know that you'll make it through this, and things will get better once again. The danger of losing sight of your commitment to each other is you can get caught up in the moment and begin to think, say, and do things that you will later regret.

When long-term perspective is lost, the relationship can quickly veer into a downward spiral. I know of couples that have lost their ability to see anything objectively. Arguments are not resolved and begin to bleed into one another. Walls have formed that are so high and thick that they no longer see their partner for who they really are. Instead, they only see problems and issues. She no longer sees the man she loves; she sees only the man who lied to her. He doesn't see his bride; he sees the woman who insists on controlling him. These points may be valid, but the priority has shifted from the relationship to the problem. Neither takes the time to remember that this was the person with whom they fell in love and committed to spend the rest of their life with. Instead, all that is seen is a thin veneer of fault and badness. Over time, that veneer becomes a solid object that contains none of the goodness and blessing that once existed.

Discussion Topics/Questions

- In a time of peace, talk with your spouse about this. Are you committed for the long run? Make that vow to one another. When conflict arises, remind yourself and each other of this fact. Knowing that you are ultimately on the same side goes a long way toward resolution.

- What is your natural approach toward conflict? Do you avoid it or address it head-on? How does that compare with your spouse?

- Think back to past arguments that you've had with your spouse. What are some key words or phrases that you heard that really frustrate you?

- Begin your list of rules of engagement for conflict situations. Are there three or four points that you can both agree to? Write these down and commit to abide by them during your next conflict.

- Agree what each of you will do when the other calls foul during an argument. Commit to doing your best at honoring that.

Weathering Life's Storms

Consider it pure joy, my brothers and sisters, whenever
you face trials of many kinds, because you know
that the testing of your faith produces perseverance.
Let perseverance finish its work so that you may
be mature and complete, not lacking anything.

—James 1:2–4 (NIV)

In 2011, National Geographic launched the television show *Doomsday Preppers*. Each episode focused on individuals or families preparing for some type of future cataclysmic event. While the nature of their concerns varied widely, everything from total government collapse, to global medical pandemics and massive natural disasters, they all had one thing in common. They were dedicated to preparing for a future state where safe food, water, and shelter would not be commonly available. While some may call these people crazy or paranoid, there is an idea for our marriages buried in the extreme prepper mind-set.

In a time of calm and normalcy, prepare for a future that might be fraught with danger and scarcity.

None of us can know what will happen tomorrow, but there are things we can and should do to prepare our marriage to weather the inevitable storms of life. Weather-related storms range in size and severity; some are forecasted while others just pop-up out of nowhere. No matter where you live, you have surely endured some type of storm. The storms we face in life and in our marriages act very much the same.

James 1:2 uses the phrase, "Whenever you face trials." Not *if* you face trials but *when* you face trials. James knew that all of us would encounter hardship, so his encouragement is to "consider it joy" because God is going to use those experiences to grow our faith. In marriage, we need to simultaneously rely on God and support our spouse during trials. In a time of calm, we can create rules of engagement that will help us remember that we are a team headed for a common goal. We can build our marriage on a firm foundation so that we can support each other during times of individual weakness and together seek the joy that only God can provide.

Tara and I have been through our share of storms, big and small. Now we can look back and see how God used those trials to grow our individual faith and to strengthen our marriage. But in the midst of the dark moments, it was much harder to see any possible benefit or to experience any type of joy. I would love to tell you that we had rules of engagement in place before our storms arrived, but that would be untrue.

Having a marriage built on rock will go a long way toward protecting you when storms occur. It is also helpful, once you've come through a trial, to reflect and consider what it is that you have learned and how that can apply to future events. The rules you create will be based upon experiences that you encounter during your marriage. I'll list the rules that we developed after we experienced these life-altering events.

Coping with the Unthinkable

October 5, 1995 was the single worst day of our lives. I was walking down the hall at work and heard my name being repeatedly paged on the office-wide intercom. Since the intercom was seldom used, I realized something unusual was going on. As I walked into my office, my assistant looked at me in panic and told me that I needed to get home immediately. It was something about my two-year-old daughter. I didn't stick around to ask questions; I could tell by her face that this was serious. I ran from the office and headed for home. What was normally a twenty-minute drive, I accomplished in ten.

As I pulled up to our house, all I could see were flashing lights, police, fire trucks, and ambulances. Neighbors were standing in the street with their hands over their mouths. Someone pointed me toward the backyard, and I ran. Within moments, I heard Tara sobbing uncontrollably then found her in the yard behind our home, kneeling near a pond, holding our two-year-old daughter Allison, limp and unmoving. Filled with horror and in a state of shock, I had no idea what to do, nor could I imagine what had occurred.

As the day went on, the details became clearer. Our daughter had gotten out the back door of our home, probably following a cat that she saw outside. She made her way up a steep hill behind our house and fell into a neighbor's pond where she drowned. When Tara noticed Allison was missing (within minutes), she immediately called the police and began a frantic search, only to discover the unthinkable had happened.

The days following this tragic event were a blur. Family, friends, and ministers flowed through the house bringing food and offering comfort. Their outreach and support were critical in getting us through this crisis. Over two hundred people came to the visitation and the funeral. In my numb state, I couldn't fathom the crowd. Most of these people had never even met our daughter. It wasn't until much later that I realized God had sent these people to comfort Tara and me.

Reality hits once the crowds have gone home. Our friends and families all resumed their respective routines. But life for us was forever changed. It was hard to eat, hard to converse, even hard to parent our older two children. We were angry. Angry with each other, angry with the neighbor who owned the pond, even angry at God. Okay, we were especially angry with God. Life progressed as if in slow motion.

After a couple of weeks, I returned to work and threw myself back into my job. It served as a distraction and allowed me to regain some sense of normalcy. As a stay-at-home mom, this was a luxury that Tara did not have. With the older boys back in school, Tara faced a suddenly empty house that was a constant reminder of Allison's absence. Life was moving on for me. For Tara, it had all but stopped.

In the weeks that followed, I found myself moving through the grieving process faster than Tara, which caused friction between us. While I felt sympathy for her and did my best to empathize, I began to resent her withdrawal from the family. Her depression led her to sleep far more than normal, leaving housework, laundry, and cooking undone. Our older boys complained that Mom didn't play with them anymore. While I missed my daughter horribly, I began to miss having a wife and a mother for our sons. As a husband, I wanted to fix the situation and make things better. But I didn't know where to start.

A couple of months after the funeral, we received a letter in the mail from an out-of-town friend. She had just learned of the accident and was sending us a belated condolence. The bulk of her letter contained scripture and words of encouragement all aimed at providing us comfort. Toward the end of the letter, she wrote that a high percentage of couples that go through such a tragedy end up getting divorced. She encouraged us to stay strong as a couple, stay close to God and to hold each other tightly throughout this season. She assured us that she would be praying for us during this time.

At first, her words made both of us furious. Why would anyone plant such a thought in our minds? How terribly insensitive! But as we reflected on the letter in the following days, our anger began to subside. We started to feel the spiritual prompting behind her efforts. When we looked at our situation honestly, there were forces beginning to pry Tara and I apart. I was moving on with life and my career as best I could, but Tara seemed stuck in that tragic moment. Both of us were growing frustrated with the other because we were grieving so differently. Our friend's letter served as a godly reminder that our relationship was built on rock, not on sand. While this was a terrible storm, we were committed to surviving it.

We had no specific Rules of Engagement that prepared us for this season. No one plans for such an event, and no one could predict exactly how they would react if faced with such a situation. But the fact that we had made commitments to each other and to our faith ultimately pulled us through. As time passed, we were able to reflect and learn how we cope with tragedy individually and as a couple.

Rule of Engagement: We will accept the people God sends into our lives to minister to us.

Thankfully, Tara and I had already developed a deep faith when Allison died. But we considered ourselves self-sufficient. We volunteered at church, took other people meals when in need and did other acts of "Christian service." But we never considered needing or accepting help ourselves. When we hit rock-bottom emotionally, we had no choice but to accept the love and service of people around us. It was easy to accept help from our very close group of friends and family, but God opened the door to many others that we needed as well. Lou, the youth minister from our church (whom we'd never met personally) came the day of the accident and just sat with us. He came back every day for a couple of weeks to do the same. He had no special healing words that he thrust upon us; rather, he was just there. His presence became a tremendous comfort, and a special relationship was formed. Twenty years later, Lou and his family are some of our closest and most trusted friends.

Rule of Engagement: We will discern between godly advice and worldly advice.

The advice we received from our Christian friends was for the most part welcomed and highly valuable. But there were many nonbelieving friends who wanted to help as well. One person told us of having just read *The Wizard of Oz* and how the lessons there could guide us in the days ahead. Another secular grief counselor brought us an old tennis racket. She suggested that when we were angry or down, we should take the racket out and swing it hard against a tree. The racket went straight into the trash as soon as she left our home.

Unfortunately, not all questions or advice from Christians is necessarily godly. Not long after the funeral, Tara got a phone call from a lady at our church. We didn't know her well but she called to offer comfort. Near the end of the otherwise pleasant conversation, she asked Tara, "What sin do you think you committed that prompted God to do this?" Tara couldn't believe her ears. The lady went on to say that she needed to know so that she could make sure she didn't commit a similar sin in her own life! Learn to discern.

Rule of Engagement: We will use our life experiences to benefit others.

God used our tragedy in a mighty way. I began to speak to various churches and other organizations telling our story, sharing that there is no guarantee in living another day. We need to make sure that we are prepared for our inevitable demise, no matter when it comes. The experience also birthed our marriage workshops. Our loss became a springboard to invite others to accept Christ into their own lives and to strengthen their marriages. I remain convinced that someday in heaven, I will meet many people who will point to our little girl's story and credit that for their conversion or for their restored marriage. Handing our crisis to God and committing to each other grew both our faith and our perseverance.

Unfortunately, trials are seldom one and done. You never know when tough times will hit. Building and maintaining a shocking marriage will equip you to handle whatever is thrown your way.

Rebuilding the Family

A couple of years after Allison's death, Tara and I had an interesting conversation during a long car ride. I remember looking at Tara and saying, "I realize that we can never replace Allison. But I do believe that we can and need to replace the role of daughter in our lives." I knew this was God-inspired when Tara looked at me and replied, "I've been thinking the exact same thing." At a recent doctor's appointment, she had been told that she probably wouldn't be able to get pregnant again. So we began to talk about adoption. I had spent considerable time on business in India and felt such compassion for orphaned children there who had no real hope for the future. I raised this as a possible location that we should consider, and Tara quickly agreed. We made the decision that we would adopt from India and began the process.

By now our sons were eight and eleven. Tara didn't want to have a single child so much younger than her siblings, so we set out to adopt sisters. We were filled with excitement as we began the process early in 1998. We filled out all of the paperwork, hosted the home visits, submitted our fingerprints, and paid the up-front fee. We even paid a premium for expedited service so that we could get the addition to our family as soon as possible.

Within a couple of months, we received pictures of two beautiful little sisters named Hema and Jyothi, aged two and three respectively. We immediately agreed to accept them and began to pray for them as we awaited their imminent arrival.

That's when our new trial began. The process dragged on as we experienced delay after delay. We were told this was not unusual when adopting from India, so we should just remain patient. We continued to pray for these two little girls and for our family. Every time we received word of another issue, we would become discouraged, but we firmly believed that God was in control, so we held on to His promise.

A year after we started the adoption process, we moved back to our hometown near Indianapolis. I had started my own business, and we wanted to be closer to our extended family. We had just completed the design of our new home when Tara found out she was pregnant! Suddenly, we were growing from a family with two kids to a soon to be family with five. "We're going to need to build a bigger house," we both agreed. So we worked with the architect and added a bedroom to the design.

Just a couple of months before the house was complete, Tara began having complications with her pregnancy and eventually had a miscarriage. While we hadn't planned this pregnancy, the loss was indescribable. It brought up all the feelings of losing Allison, and it felt like the pain was compounded. Again, we relied on each other and on God to get through this time. We began to question God as to what was going on and why.

In the spring of 2000, we moved into our new house, complete with a bedroom decorated for our Indian girls. It felt like a fresh start. Even in the midst of the excitement and anticipation, we were still no closer to completing the adoption. While we continued to pray for the arrival of our Indian daughters, we received an unexpected blessing. Tara was pregnant again, and in January 2002, our son Jacob was born.

Just before Jacob's first birthday, we got word from the adoption agency that the Indian government had shut down the orphanage where Hema and Jyothi were being raised. It stemmed from a local journalistic accusation that was later proved to be unfounded. But in any case, the two little girls we considered a part of our family were taken away, never to be seen or heard of again.

To us, this was a third form of losing a child (in this case, children). Our anger and despair was greater than ever. Every time we would walk past their empty bedroom, we were reminded of the promise that never came to fruition. Maintaining our faith became harder than ever before. This felt like an all-out spiritual conspiracy against us, and it pushed our relationship with God and with each other to the limit.

In the depths of our mourning, we were reminded that as difficult as it was, God had gotten us through our past experiences, and His promise was that He would get us through this one as well. We began to come out of our individual silos of despair and once again pulled together in conversation and prayer. We accepted we would once again have three children. This season led to new rules of engagement that have served as ongoing reminder in more recent storms.

Rule of Engagement: We will believe together that God can sustain us through any situation.

Rule of Engagement: We will respect and support each other as we grieve differently.

Rule of Engagement: We will keep lines of communication open between ourselves and with God even in the toughest of times.

Right after we celebrated Jacob's second birthday, we received an unexpected phone call from a social worker from Washington, DC. Our adoption file had been transferred to his office, and he had identified a new little girl (from India) for us, and he wanted to confirm our interest in continuing with the process. We couldn't believe our ears! We assumed that once the orphanage closed, our adoption prospects had ended. We had no idea that anyone was still trying to find a child for us. While our hearts still ached for the loss of the original sisters, we almost immediately agreed to proceed with this new child.

Later that year, we adopted the most beautiful little Indian girl we'd ever seen. Her birthday was also in January, just a week before Jacob's. It wasn't until we celebrated both of their birthdays for the first time that we realized "Hey, look, we have siblings aged two and three. Wasn't that the original intent?" God's ways are not always our ways. We had four children aged seventeen, fourteen, three, and two. Going back to my roots of being raised on a farm, we began to affectionately refer to them as our spring crop and our fall crop of kids. To this day, we still find ourselves praying for Hema and Jyothi. There's no way to find out what became of them, but we sincerely hope to see them in heaven one day.

Rule of Engagement: We will trust in God's plan for our lives, even when it differs from our own.

We have a fantastic, tight-knit family. It's not one that we could have ever imagined or planned for, but we see it as a pure blessing from God. In times of uncertainty since this season, we have learned to trust in God even when the way forward is not obvious.

Financial Hardship

The Great Recession hit my business hard in the fall of 2007. I had built it up to a nine-person company and was beginning to be recognized as an industry leader. Our focus was on the very front-end of new product development, meaning that we helped companies to develop ideas and strategies that they could implement in the future. Over the course of a few weeks, our work suddenly dried up completely. We went from managing four to five projects at a time to zero.

Based on the hint of a forthcoming recession, our target clients stopped investing in this area, opting instead to sit on their cash and spend only on near-term necessities. As a result, our company was hit much earlier than others. While the word recession was being bantered about on television and news magazines, the effects were not commonly seen yet. I had friends who were business owners who claimed their companies were booming. I assumed that it was just a blip, and that things would simply come back if I remained patient and steadfast.

The team I had assembled were like family, and I held on to them much longer than I should have. By the time I let the last person go in 2008, I had gone almost six months with no revenue coming in, and payroll and other expenses going out. I'd dug a deep hole for myself. With the recession now in full swing, it was nearly impossible to see a way out.

Through renegotiation with lenders and investment by extended family members, I was ultimately able to keep the business open. But during the worst of that season, I had to put myself on unemployment for almost six months. I feared losing my house and everything else that I owned. I felt like a complete failure both as a business owner and as a husband. One day as I was going through the mail, I came across a life insurance statement. It took no time at all to realize that I was worth considerably more dead than alive. I didn't contemplate suicide, but horrible, negative thoughts did begin to flood my mind. Why would Tara stay with me? Didn't she deserve better? She was going through this season along with me and was aware of our unpaid bills and threatening debt collectors. Yet she had a peace and a calmness that I could not seem to muster. The last thing that I wanted to do was to ruin her demeanor by sharing my concerns and fears. Not talking about it seemed better than getting into a highly uncomfortable conversation. Though my intent was to display an attitude of faith and strength, she saw right through it.

One day, I broke down in front of her. The stress was just too much for me to bear. Not only was I not being a good provider; now I was a sobbing weak man. When I finally settled down, she looked me in the eye and very calmly asked me, "What is the worst that could happen?"—a question that infuriated me. Was she in complete denial? I looked at her in shock and responded something to the effect of "I'll tell you the worst that could happen. We can lose our house. We'll have to declare bankruptcy. Life as we know it will be over. We'll have to live under a bridge!"

She sat directly across from me, put her hands on my knees, looked me right in the eye and said, "If that happens, then we'll live under a bridge together." I could never express how much that brief sentence meant to me, but it completely changed my perspective. In that moment, I was able to separate our situation, which was temporary, from our relationship, which was committed and lasting. I realized we were in this situation together, and no matter what the outcome might be, our marriage would stay intact. I no longer carried the burden alone. She shared it with me. We began to pray together and plan various contingencies. When we had nowhere else to turn and had given the entire situation to God, things began to change for the better. My phone started to ring, and work started to come back in. God had sustained us through another trial. I thank God for his provision and for Tara's inspirational faith.

Creating Rules of Engagement to Get Through Trials

I pray that you never have to go through the loss of a child or severe financial strain, but every marriage will experience trials of some variety. Are you prepared? The devil wants nothing more than to separate you from your strongest supporters, God and your spouse, during these times. How many people do you know who have questioned God's very existence or turned away from Him as a result of a severe trial? Our friend's statistics were true: a high percentage of marriages do result in divorce after the loss of a child. Trials are the ploys of Satan to separate us from our base of strength. While a cord of three is not easily broken, a single cord can snap easily.

Committing to God and to your spouse, regardless of circumstance, is a critical step in preparing for an uncertain future. Just as the doomsday preppers are stockpiling food and water, you need to be preparing your heart and soul for potential tragedy. When you are in the midst of hardship, these commitments will go a long way toward helping you through.

Discussion Questions

- What trials have you gone through with your spouse? How did they affect your relationship?

- What did you learn about yourself from the experience? What did you learn about your spouse from the experience?

- What promises does God provide that can sustain you during trials?

- What role does communication play during trials? How does it affect your communication with God? How does it affect your communication with your spouse?

- Based on what you've learned, what rules of engagement could you create that would help you in future trials?

6

Keeping the Spark Alive

I was an Eagle Scout, and as a part of my Scout experience, I learned how to start a fire using natural materials. In that process, I came to understand that it takes considerable effort to create a spark. Once you've got a spark, you do everything possible to keep it alive until you can convert it into an actual flame. You have to gently blow on it to keep it alight until the adjoining material catches. It's quite an involved process that requires you to pay close attention to what you're doing and react based on what is happening around you. Sometimes the environment around you makes it easier (think, dry materials) and sometimes considerably harder (think wet materials on a really windy day). As a determined Scout, the goal was to get a fire going regardless of the conditions. Once the fire was lit, there was a tremendous feeling of satisfaction and accomplishment.

To this day, one of my favorite parts of camping is waking up in the morning and reigniting the remnants of the campfire from the previous night. While the fire may appear to be completely burned out, I will dig around in the charred wood looking for an ember. Once I find one, I know that with some effort, I can get the fire going again. I'll gather and add some fresh kindling, then get down on my knees and gently blow on the ember. When I see it begin to turn from ash white to glowing red, I know I'm making progress. After a short while, the fire is going again, wood can be added, and it will burn all day if I just keep tending it.

Like a campfire, there are times when our marriages are red hot and times when the heat subsides. When distractions in life pull us away from our spouse, the embers get buried. If we're committed to staying together, the fire never goes out completely, and with some effort, we can to get the fire going again. Once again, the key is intentionality.

Satisfying Unmet Needs

We all have needs. Basic physical needs (e.g., food, water, clothing, and shelter) are required for survival. A starving person will do things that were once inconsiderable in order to get nourishment. Once our basic needs have been met, we also have emotional needs (e.g., acceptance, love, friendship, empathy) and spiritual needs (e.g., the innate desire to connect with something much larger than ourselves). While we may be able to satisfy our own physical needs, we have to look beyond ourselves to satisfy our emotional and spiritual needs.

Early on in marriage, it is easy and natural to focus on your partner's needs. As the newness dissipates and comfort slips in, the attention often shifts from your partner to your own needs. You begin to evaluate your spouse in terms of how well they are pleasing you and focus on areas where they are letting you down. Disappointment sets in, and instinctively, you begin to crave fulfillment, either consciously or subconsciously.

A woman whose emotional needs are not met within marriage may turn to friends, social media, or movies. Eventually, she may become vulnerable to the attention of other men, seeking to fill the void that is lacking in her marriage.

For men, the need is typically not emotional but most often physical (sexual). Seventy percent of men aged eighteen to thirty-five admit to having been on an Internet pornography site within the last month. The sad truth is there is no measurable difference between Christian men and men who are not believers. Many justify this outlet as filling a void that their wife no longer satisfies.

I'm not excusing any of these behaviors. Sin is sin, no matter what might lead you to it. But staying focused on our spouse and their needs is one powerful way to minimize the temptations that they might otherwise face. Shifting the focus back from self to partner takes commitment and effort. It's neither easy nor natural, but it can be learned. Focus on your own behaviors and work hard to fulfill the needs of your partner. It's an interesting phenomenon. The more you work to meet their needs, the more your own needs will ultimately be met.

Fighting Complacency

We own an English bulldog. He's lazy, he snores, he drools, he can clear a room when he passes gas, and he loves to cuddle. We also have a cat. She's a typical cat, showing no interest in anyone who wants to play with her and ceaselessly tormenting any noncat lovers who happen by. We got our bulldog puppy when the cat was about eight years old. These two have developed an interesting relationship. While they were mortal enemies at first, they don't really fight anymore. They just coexist. The cat will be in the room with us until she sees the dog approaching, then she casually exits for another part of the house. If the dog happens to notice her, he might growl a little. But for the most part, that requires too much energy. They appear to have agreed upon a mutual avoidance strategy. Both feel they deserve to be in the room, but they choose not to be around each other.

While amusing in the animal world, it's very sad when this behavior is replicated in marriage. I know too many couples that live this way, coexisting in the same space, moving from room to room while avoiding eye contact. They're often past fighting, certainly past loving but stay together out of habit or convenience.

This does not happen overnight. Relationships have natural ups and downs. Couples go through phases where they are crazy about each other, and through phases where they drive each other crazy. Shocking marriages look past the momentary feelings and rely on the promised long-term commitment. Beyond that, they are proactive when they find themselves edging toward complacency and do something to reinvigorate the relationship.

We fall into patterns of laziness and routine with our spouse because they are comfortable, predictable, and—let's face it—easy. Comfort and predictability may sound desirable, but when carried to an extreme, they lead to boredom and discontent, which are very dangerous. Marriages in this condition are extremely vulnerable to others who might offer more excitement and attention. Let me state it clearly.

Complacency Is the Enemy of a Shocking Marriage!

It's amazing how much effort we put on making a great impression on strangers or people we barely know. There's much truth in the old saying: "You only have one opportunity to make a great first impression." First impressions go a long way and may last a long time. In a marriage, we are making impressions on our spouse every time we're together. If our ongoing actions don't support their first impression, their perception of us will change over time. There is beauty in the comfort that comes with an ongoing intimate relationship. We should be able to say and do things in front of our spouse that we would never consider doing in front of others. When comfort becomes complacency, or when we stop caring what impression we are making on them, the relationship will begin to erode.

Picture this. Wives, you are at a business function with your husband. You stand loyally at his side throughout the evening and thoroughly enjoy the charm, the warmth, and the conversation that he exudes with everyone he encounters. You see a facet of him that you absolutely adore, a side that caused you to fall in love in the first place. But you feel torn. You ask yourself, "Is this the same man who won't look up from the television when I'm trying to talk with him? Is this charmer the same guy who burps at dinner and grunts a reply when I ask a question? What happened to the man I married?"

Flip side. Husbands, you attend a social charity event with your wife. You are quite taken back when she emerges from the bathroom looking like a model. She's dressed to kill. Her hair is stunning.

Her makeup perfectly applied. You couldn't be more proud to be her husband as you notice the other men taking a second glance at her throughout the evening. Having the most beautiful wife at the party makes you stand a little taller. You feel confident and aroused at the same time. The next day at work, you can't stop thinking about her and can't wait to get home. However, when you walk in the house, your fantasy is shattered. She's wearing sweat pants, a ratty T-shirt, and her hair is a mess. She tells you how proud she is that she's been deep cleaning the bathrooms all afternoon.

Why is it that we act and dress for success with mere acquaintances but take our spouse for granted so much of the time? Why do we care so much about what others think while completely ignoring how we portray ourselves to the person we love the most?

Let me share with you a great real-life positive example. Several years ago, my sister-in-law and her kids were visiting from out of state, and we had been playing around our pool all day. My brother, her husband, was due to fly in from a business trip and join us that evening. As late afternoon approached, she quietly slipped away leaving her kids in the pool with our family. She went in to the house, showered, put on nice clothes, makeup and did her hair. When she came back outside, I was surprised at her transformation and asked her if they were going out somewhere? I'll never forget her response, "No. But Jim (her husband) will be here soon, so I did this for him." "Why?" I asked. Without hesitation, she replied, "He's been traveling all week. He's been around beautiful, professional women at the office, and I want to look my best for him when he gets here." She didn't do this out of fear or paranoia, but with a sense of joy and anticipation.

My brother and sister-in-law have a shocking marriage, and it's one that Tara and I have tried to model in many ways. There's nothing wrong with dressing up and acting our best for other people, but we should be willing to do that for our spouses upon occasion as well. A solid relationship should be one where we can truly be ourselves and feel both safe and comfortable. However, we must avoid becoming so comfortable and self-centered that we consistently put our own needs ahead of our partner's. A healthy relationship requires a balance in this area. What my sister-in-law showed us was that she gave her husband intentional priority over the other relationships that surrounded her. This resulted in a new rule of engagement for us.

Rule of Engagement: I will not take my spouse or their needs for granted.

Prioritizing with Kids

Giving your spouse priority is difficult, especially once kids enter the picture. We live in a kid-focused culture where lives often revolve around the desires, needs, and schedules of our children. Obviously, there are seasons where this may be required. A newborn will not patiently wait for Mom and Dad to finish their conversation before loudly declaring their hunger. But as kids get older and gain some self-sufficiency it is important that they learn to respect that mommy and daddy need time together. I've heard it said that "good kids don't make a great marriage, but a great marriage can make good kids." One of the greatest gifts we can give our kids is a solid marriage where love and respect are modeled between spouses.

I'm amazed at how few couples set aside any time for date nights without the kids. Many couples we've met have *never* gotten a babysitter! In our conversations, it was often the mother who was reluctant to commit to a date night, mentioning the guilt she would feel leaving the kids behind even for an evening.

This attitude can communicate a variety of messages. The husband hears, "While you used to be my primary focus in life, now that we have children, you are being placed on the back burner. I'll get back to you someday." The children hear, "You are the most important people in Mommy's life. Daddy is here to help me meet all of your needs." And those outside of, but close to, the marriage hear, "I needed him to give me these kids. They're my everything now." All these messages are troubling and outside of God's design for marriage.

Our marriages thrive when we have distinct priorities. First is our relationship with God, second is our relationship with our spouse, and third is our relationship with our kids. When any of these get out of order, problems arise. In the pool example, my sister-in-law left the kids behind with Tara and I when she went in to change. She knew the kids were safe, and she made the choice to stop playing with them to prepare herself for her husband. Her priority was clear! Helping your children understand your priorities is critical. It allows them to see where they fit in in terms of the natural order of things. Our kids knew that if Tara and I were in a serious conversation, they needed to wait to interrupt to get our attention. I appreciated when Tara would look at them and say, "Mommy and Daddy are talking right now. If this is not an emergency, you need to wait." It communicated to me that I was her priority, and it communicated to the kids that our relationship was of key importance.

Just as setting aside regular time for a date night is important, setting aside smaller amounts of time on a more frequent basis is also important. One thing that we did was implement an ongoing event that we called Martini Mondays. This amounted to setting aside thirty minutes when I got home from work on Monday when we would sit on our front porch, the back deck, or somewhere else intentional and have Mommy and Daddy time. We might drink a martini, or it might be a glass of iced tea, but our goal was making time to talk and reconnect. Before long, the kids learned that we did not want to be disturbed during that time, and they came to respect it. Traditionally, there's so little to like about Mondays, but we made it our favorite day of the week.

Rule of Engagement: God gets first priority, but my spouse gets second.

Rule of Engagement: We will set aside time together on a regular basis.

Keep Their Glass Full

This may sound strange coming from a guy, but I love weddings. I learn something from every single wedding I attend. It's a great chance to watch and talk with people from many backgrounds and with many views on marriage. It's like a living laboratory. Tara and I recently went to a family wedding. The venue was outdoors at a downtown museum, the weather was perfect, and it was great to see extended family that we had not seen in a long time. Between the ceremony and the reception was a cocktail hour with an open bar and served appetizers. At one point, the two of us were standing at a table and talking when one of the servers came up offering an hors d'oeuvre. She noticed that Tara's drink was almost gone. She looked directly at me and said, "Mhmm, mmmh…You need to keep your lady's glass full if you know what's good for you." We all laughed as she walked away. But I couldn't get those words out of my mind for the rest of the evening.

Her comment had many profound implications. In a literal sense, it would simply be polite of me to offer her a refill before she had to ask. Beyond that, the glass could represent Tara's life or state of mind. Before it would occur to me to keep Tara's glass full, I would have to notice that her glass is nearly empty. That would require me to pay sufficient attention to assess the situation and anticipate her needs before they become too great. Her needs clearly go beyond thirst. Knowing my wife better than anyone else on earth should allow me to notice and anticipate her other needs as well.

Keeping her glass full could imply filling an emotional need. If I'm focused, I can detect when she is angry, frustrated, uncomfortable, or frightened without her having to tell me. I see that she is getting nervous before she panics or that she's upset before she becomes angry. Putting out a small fire is far easier than extinguishing a major blaze.

Keeping her glass full could even mean meeting a physical need. There are times when I can tell she just needs a hug, and providing that can be far more beneficial than I could ever imagine. Maybe I notice that she's really tired, and I simply jump in to help her on a task she's working on. There have been times when I've come into the house and within minutes take the kids out to play because it's obvious that she needs a break from them.

Noticing a need is a crucial first step, but proactively satisfying it is of even more importance. In our thirty-five years of marriage, there have been times when I have noticed her needs (an emptying glass) but have been too self-absorbed or busy to do anything about it. You get no points for detection if you don't follow up with a solution. It is important to stop, notice the emptying glass, and take the time to refill it.

I'll never know if that waitress was simply suggesting that I get my wife another drink or if she was pointing me toward a far more profound learning. In either case, it was a great reminder.

Speak Their Love Language

A very practical way of keeping your spouse's glass full is to speak their love language. In his 1995 book *Love Languages*, Gary Chapman says that each of us has one of five primary love languages: quality time, words of affirmation, acts of service, gifts, and physical touch. Each of these represents a distinct manner in which we naturally want to show and be shown love. If you've not read his book, I strongly encourage you to do so. This is a very simple, yet effective step in focusing on each other's needs.

When I was in corporate life, I had a job with global responsibilities. As a result, I traveled extensively on an international basis. A typical trip would span two weeks and three weekends. Traveling to exotic places around the world was very exciting, but it was tough on both Tara and I to be gone so much of the time.

Every time I would go to a new place, my first thought was how much I wished that Tara could be with me. With her on my mind, I would consistently set aside some time during the trip to find her something special that I could give to her upon my return. I'm not talking about picking up a souvenir at the airport. No way. I would find a local colleague and ask what specifically would represent that particular area in terms of a gift for my wife. I would then determine a way to procure such an item personally to make sure it was perfect for her. This might have been an opal from Australia or inlaid marble art from India.

One time in China, I heard about a very rare variety of loose-leaf tea that could only be bought in the region where I was visiting. That afternoon, before I headed to the airport, I found myself riding in an open three-wheeled motorized cart, zipping through crowded streets at breakneck speed to a specific teashop where this tea was sold. I bought a tin of tea from an old Chinese man with only two teeth who didn't speak a word of English. I just knew that Tara would love it.

Fast-forward forty hours, I walk in the front door of my house, jet-lagged and exhausted. My kids swarm me and are giddy with excitement. Tara gives me a big hug to welcome me home. After an hour of catching up, I headed off to take a shower. "Don't take too long," Tara told me. "I've made a nice dinner for you."

Once I emerged from the shower, more tired now than ever, I dug through my bag to grab the gift-wrapped tin of tea. I couldn't wait to give it to her and tell her the story behind it. I took it downstairs and saw that everyone was already seated at the table waiting for me. I sat down, then handed Tara the tea, excited to see her reaction. She was appreciative, but set it on the side table and said, "Let's eat." I was disappointed at her lack of reaction, but I could barely keep my eyes open since my brain was off by ten hours. I really enjoyed eating with the family again but found it hard to eat too much in my jet-lagged state. Once dinner was over, I retired to the living room and promptly fell asleep in front of the television.

This story played out numerous times over the course of about six years. It wasn't until we read the *Love Languages* that we discovered that my primary love language was "gifts" and hers was "acts of service." I'll never forget the conversation that ensued. "You mean all those things that you brought back for me was your way of expressing love? I just assumed you grabbed something you saw that you thought was interesting," Tara stated. I affirmed that is exactly what my gestures meant and told her some of the more interesting stories of the effort I had extended to get some of the gifts. She had no idea. She actually began to weep a bit.

Then it hit me. "Wait a second, those big meals you made for me when I got home, that was your expression of love?" Of course it was. I had no idea of the time and effort she had put in to the preparation of those special meals. Being exhausted and having eaten at expensive restaurants for two straight weeks led me to underappreciate what she was offering. But in that moment, I realized it was never about the food—it was about her effort in preparing something special for me to enjoy.

Until we understood this concept, we assumed that we both expressed love in the same manner. Knowing your partner's love language and speaking it are very strong expressions of selflessness and consideration. I continued to buy gifts, and Tara continued to make great meals, but we never took them for granted again.

When you speak your partner's love language, you are showing that you are willing to make an effort to put their interests first. The first time I went to France, my coworkers warned me that the French can be quite snobbish if you don't speak their language. While I've never been fluent in any language (including English, according to some of my high school teachers!), I made an effort to speak a few key phrases in French while at hotels or in restaurants. I was amazed at the change of attitude I saw once I extended this effort. While I feared I would be ridiculed for my lack of linguistics, the exact opposite occurred. The French hospitality staff appreciated me making the effort and went considerable distance to assist me in my requests. The same is true in your marriage. Your efforts will show intent and serve as an expression of true love.

Be Intentional

There are a lot of elements involved in keeping the spark alive within your marriage. Committing to a stronger marriage involves an ongoing effort and must supersede day-to-day feelings. Shocking marriages hold on to their commitments of continuous growth even during the low seasons. They recognize that downtimes are only temporary, and that better days lie just around the corner. I've heard economy experts say that the best time to invest in the stock market is during a recession. Prices are low, but they will inevitably rebound. Investments during these times have tremendous rates of return. Marriage is no different. Investing in a night away or in a special date night can convert the blasé feelings into excitement and even passion.

One of the ways we are intentional is in setting annual goals. We go out to dinner to celebrate our anniversary, and one of my favorite parts of the evening is when we reflect on the past year of marriage and proactively plan for the upcoming year. We'll talk about highs and lows and discuss areas where we've grown closer and areas where we've drifted a bit. Even after thirty-plus years of marriage, I still make a lot of assumptions about how Tara perceives things (and vice versa). Something that I think went really well, she may have perceived as falling short. Then we'll shift our thinking to the coming year. What is it we would love to accomplish in the next year of marriage? What do we want to change? While the primary focus is specifically on shared goals within our relationship, we also talk about goals that we have as individuals. We express love when we support each other in these pursuits. Dreaming about the future bonds us together. Accomplishing our goals or not is far less important than taking the time to talk together and plan for the future. It's harder to drift apart if you regularly ensure you are headed toward the same future goal.

Rule of Engagement: We will regularly assess our relationship and proactively plan for the future.

Discussion Questions

- Look back at your marriage with your spouse (for the past month, year, five years—whatever is applicable). Describe some times when you felt like your relational fire was really roaring. What did that look like? What did it feel like? What were some of the specific events/activities that were taking place during that time?

- Look back over the same time period. Describe some times when you felt like your relational fire was dwindling. What did that look like? How did that feel? What were the situations in your relationship during that time?

- Consider what took place that either caused your fire to either grow or diminish.

- What are some tangible warning signs that your fire may be fading? What are some specific actions you can take to stoke it back up?

- What rules of engagement could you create to help keep you aware and on track in this area?

- What are your respective love languages (if you are not sure, take a free online test at 5lovelanguages.com to see)? How well do you "speak" your spouse's love language? How could you do this more effectively?

- Think of one to two goals you would like to pursue over the next year to keep your spark alive.

7

Intimacy

The range and diversity of perspectives that fall under the broad umbrella of Christian intimacy is incredible. As I have read books and blogs on marriage, I've discovered two things: First, what one Christian couple considers as healthy and enticing from a sexual standpoint may be condemned by another Christian couple. Second, we develop a sex life that works for us and label that as normal. The health of other marriages is then measured by how far they deviate from our personal standard. Isn't it interesting that we are all operating under the same God-given user's manual, the Bible?

My goal is not to suggest the "one right way" to express or enjoy intimacy within your marriage. God didn't make any two people or couples identical. If you were to map out all the individual physical, mental, and spiritual characteristics of each person, then factor in all of the combinations created by bringing together any couple, the number would be astronomical. That is a beautiful thing. God created sex and intimacy and intends for married couples to enjoy it and discover what best suits them. He gave us His Word for direction and gave us the community of other believers for support.

I think there is beauty and power in sharing practices and perspectives. While no other couple may be exactly like us, they may face similar struggles. No two couples should develop the same rules of engagement for intimacy, but rules in this area should not be ignored.

Creating guidelines for intimacy allows you to give this area of your marriage proper consideration so that over time, it won't be neglected.

The Game with No Winners

In the workshops Tara and I have led, numerous men have vented to us about the lack of sex in their marriage. "My wife is always too tired, doesn't feel well, or just isn't in the mood. It's maddening." Many will go on to express that they feel completely at their wife's mercy when it comes to their sexual relationship. These husbands may be the head of the household in other areas, but when it comes to intimacy, they find themselves having to bargain or even plead for sex. "When we do have sex, it's completely up to her, when, where, and how. I have little say in the matter. But I'm afraid to complain or bring it up in conversation for risk of being cut off even more."

Conversely, women routinely complain about the lack of non-sexual attention they get from their husbands. "Why can't my husband just hold me? Why does it always have to lead to sex? I don't mind sex, but that shouldn't be the only time that he will touch me." This inevitably becomes a self-fulfilling prophecy. When he does reach out to put his arm around her, or give her a kiss, she immediately assumes that he is trying to seduce her. Finding this offensive, she gives him the (typically nonverbal) message that she is not interested in sex, which in turn drives him away.

Behaviors such as these don't always fall so cleanly along gender lines. Sometimes it's the wife with the stronger sexual drive, and the husband is less interested. While the roles may sometimes be reversed, the tension remains the same. If one spouse rejects their partner's advances long enough, eventually they may quit offering any kind of physical attention at all. Over time, these feelings of rejection are detrimental to the relationship. For the purpose of simplicity in this chapter, I will go with the assumption that the man has the stronger drive. Feel free to reverse the roles when applicable.

Is it possible to satisfy the needs of both partners when they're so seemingly different? The answer is yes, but it requires a new mind-set for each person. In this area, more than others, men and women are wired differently. A 1995 study conducted by the Kinsey Institute showed that 54 percent of men thought about sex several times per day. Only 19 percent of women thought about sex even once a day. This study was an average of men and women of all ages. It's probably safe to assume that the numbers are even higher for men in their prime physical years.

We inherently and unintentionally create the relationship situation in which we're living. Both genders are often guilty of baiting and switching through the transition from dating to marriage. Dating men may buy expensive gifts for their girlfriends. They may be willing to sit and talk for hours. Strolling down the beach hand in hand? Of course! That is until they actually marry, at which time many of these seductive behaviors quickly dissipate. Likewise, if a couple is sexually active prior to marriage, it is not uncommon for the woman to say or do various things in an effort to "catch" a husband. Once he's on the hook, her personal preferences kick in, and these lures also go away. Every marriage goes through a passionate honeymoon phase where a couple just can't seem to get enough of each other, but this phase doesn't last forever.

Once the honeymoon phase subsides, unhealthy behaviors may kick in. Many women use sex as a reward for behavior they want to encourage or withhold it as punishment for undesired behavior. "If he buys me flowers, I'll give him sex," or "He's not going to get any tonight based on the comment he made this morning." Over time, the husband adapts to certain patterns. Sex is a strong motivator for men, and they will naturally take the path of least resistance to get it. Even when they know they are being manipulated, they will often play the game to achieve their end goal.

Guys, on the other hand, are always looking for an opening to advance sex. If the wife cozies up next to him on the couch, there's physical contact. "Aha! Here's my chance" is the first thought that comes to his mind. "If I just touch her in the right places in the right sequence, she's sure to want sex. At least that used to work." He spends his emotional energy trying to sell her on the idea of sex, but ultimately, she's the buyer. If she doesn't pull the trigger to initiate the sale, he gets frustrated and grumpy. She knows this and comes to learn the minimum frequency she needs to say yes to keep him from going off the deep end. And the ugly, frustrating game continues.

Changing the Rules

Before we began offering marriage workshops, our pastor led a series on sexuality in marriage. He discussed biblical examples of healthy sexual attitudes as seen in Song of Solomon and the consequences of unhealthy behaviors, such as David and Bathsheba. In the last week of the series, he pointed out that in our modern times, we've developed a warped perspective on sex. 1 Corinthians 7:4–5 instructs us that the only time either partner in a marriage should withhold sex from the other is when both partners have agreed to abstain and, then, only for a brief period of prayer and fasting. He went on to say that "Not tonight, I have a headache," or "The kids have been rotten today, I just can't," or "I'm just not in the mood" are not scripturally valid reasons for a partner to say no. He went on to say that if the husband is following the biblical model of marriage, he would be in tune with his wife enough to understand and respect those times when he can see that the situation is not ideal for sex. He told us that that in our Christian culture, women may allow their husbands to be the head of the household in most areas, but when it comes to having sex, most retain absolute control. He challenged the ladies of our church to not say no without good reason.

It felt like a long walk out of the church that morning with my mind reeling from the sermon. Tara and I had a great marriage, but honestly, sex was the one ongoing issue that led to conflict and hurt feelings. Just as our pastor had described, I felt like this was one area I was completely subject to her whims, moods, and desires. When I would bring up my desire for intimacy, it would often end in an argument with both of us justifying our perspectives. My fear was that this sermon had angered her, so I was determined to avoid the topic.

As we began to drive away from the church, Tara calmly asked me, "What did you think of the sermon?" While this was not an atypical question, I wanted to change the subject as quickly as I could. But instead of diverting, I reversed the question and asked her, "What did you think of it?" offering no opinion of my own. Tara told me that she had never heard this scripture taught before and felt convicted by the message. "Okay," I said cautiously, "so what does that mean for us?" She sat quietly, obviously thinking and praying as I began the drive home. After a few miles, she looked at me and said, "Let's try it." Not wanting to make any stupid assumptions, and looking straight out the windshield at the road, I asked her, "Okay. What exactly do you mean by that?" She told me that for the next thirty days, she wouldn't say no when I initiated intimacy. I was stunned by this and drove for a couple of miles without saying a word. Finally, I nervously asked what she expected of me in return. Her response was something to the effect of "I don't have any conditions. I would only request that you be sensitive to me and my needs."

Much to Tara's surprise, it took me a few days to initiate sex. I don't know if I was concerned that she wasn't serious about her offer or if the "pressure" of knowing she'd say yes just flummoxed me in the short term. In any case, it turned out to be a fantastic thirty days for both of us. At the end of the time, we spoke openly about the experience. Our biggest realization was that we had both been playing unhealthy games in this regard. Specific learning included the following:

- *I traditionally requested sex more often than what I really wanted.* At a subconscious level, I figured that if I was told no two out of every three times that I requested sex, I would ask three times more than I needed it. This would improve my overall odds of getting a yes with sufficient frequency. From Tara's perspective, I asked all the time, even in ridiculous situations. Saying no to any given request was not a big deal. She knew I'd ask again soon.

- *The actual frequency of sex remained unchanged from previous months.* Tara was convinced that this month would be a throwback to early marriage. To her surprise, the actual frequency did not change much, but the tension and conflict generated from my constant nagging went away.

- *Not having to "work for it" changed my attitude toward Tara.* I found myself being more naturally physical and more attentive to her needs. I wasn't worried about getting worked up now and being frustrated later. As a result, I wouldn't hesitate to cuddle on the couch or hold her hand. My motivation for physical contact changed from trying to "get her in the mood" to simply expressing affection. I knew that if I wanted intimacy, she would agree. From her perspective, the amount of nonsexual touch that she craved increased dramatically. Knowing that sex was available at any time made me more sensitive to her current mood and situation. If I could tell she was stressed-out or very tired, I saw no reason to ask; it could wait for a better moment. This was affirming for her and became very natural to me.

- *Our petty arguments all but came to an end.* We both noticed there was less tension in our relationship. I realized that I was harboring resentment toward Tara for rejecting my requests for intimacy. This resentment would express itself as complaints about unrelated things, like the state of the house or the kid's behavior. But it was actually lashing out at her for my perceived rejection. From Tara's perspective, I started complaining the moment I came into the house, which made her resentful and less likely to agree to sex. The cycle would continue until Tara would agree to "pity sex," an act that I despised but accepted anyway. During this rejection-free month, I no longer had the feelings of frustration that would start our downward spiral, which eliminated our daily arguments.

- *The microwave/crock pot analogy is misleading.* We've all heard the analogy that men are like microwave ovens, ready for sex at a moment's notice, and that women are like Crock-Pots that heat up slowly. I took that to mean that if I wanted to have sex in the evening, I needed to work for it all day long. I would rub Tara's shoulders in the morning before I'd leave for work. I would make a special effort to call her a few times during the day and walk in the door with nothing but compliments coming from my mouth. In my mind, I had performed all of the necessary steps to all but guarantee me sex once it came time for bed. Tara's perspective was different. From the first shoulder rub in the morning, she would think, "I know what he's up to." When she answered my phone calls, in her mind she would say, "He only calls when he wants sex." By the time I arrived home with my compliments, she had decided, "I know exactly what you want, and that's just not going to happen." All of my efforts to express affection felt like manipulation, making the thought of having sex almost repulsive. Removing rejection allowed me to focus on her needs out of love rather than to earn a reward, which allowed her to freely receive my affection without feeling like there was a hidden agenda. When I request sex, she's ready, not because of what I've done the last four hours, but rather because of how I've treated her over the course of days or even weeks.

After thirty days neither wanted to go back to our old ways. What started as an experiment is now a way of life.

Rule of Engagement: Make "yes" the default answer when my partner asks for sex.

Rule of Engagement: Never use sex as a tool or associate it with power.

Sex is not a right to be demanded but a beautiful expression of love and intimacy to be enjoyed by both of us.

The Beauty of Long-Term Commitment

I've heard some single people say that they can't imagine only sleeping with one person for the rest of their lives—the boredom would be overwhelming and intolerable. These people are not looking for or following God's design for marriage, as the Bible clearly speaks of man and woman becoming "one flesh." Physical oneness through sexual intimacy is a part of the one flesh idea, but the concept doesn't stop there. As a couple lives together in holy matrimony, their two lives become one in many ways. Beyond physical intimacy, they begin to share convictions, beliefs, and even life goals. They share each other's joys and feel each other's pain. These shared traits follow right into the bedroom.

I find tremendous beauty in the fact that I know what pleases my wife. I know her likes and dislikes. In fact, I know things about her that no one else on earth could possibly know, and because of that, I feel special. These weren't learned overnight but over a series of years. The things that she loved as a twenty-something newlywed are not necessarily the same things she most appreciates now, thirty years later. Had I not evolved with her over that time, she would be highly dissatisfied with me now.

One of the greatest aspects of long-term marriage is the ability to be completely vulnerable. There is no need to put up a façade or try to pretend to be something you're not. You can share a level of honesty and openness that is not experienced in any other relationship. Unconditional love takes away fear and insecurity. Intimacy may change in form over time, but it should continue to grow in depth.

The Challenges of Long-Term Commitment

It saddens me when I hear long-married couples talk about boredom in the bedroom. My question back to them is always, "Well, whose fault is that?" Being married for a long time to the same person should lead to comfort, but not to monotony. When comfort is carried to an extreme, it becomes routine and boring. It's easy to lie in bed and follow a well-established pattern leading up to sex. Many couples could probably plot out their typical sex routine in a simple step-by-step format. First he does this, then she responds with this, then he touches her here, then she touches him there, until the act is complete. It's safe, predictable, and easy. It doesn't require a lot of thought, imagination, or effort. While this might lead to short-term physical satisfaction, it certainly leaves the mental aspect of intimacy lacking. Over time, boredom will reduce the frequency until sex becomes merely a physical release, leading to more routine sex, which leads to more mental dissatisfaction, etc. The whole process becomes a vicious cycle where no one is satisfied physically or emotionally.

Selfishness can also creep into a relationship as the initial excitement over intimacy fades. In the early stages of marriage, it is easy to focus on your partner's needs rather than your own. As you discover the likes and preferences of your partner, you are excited to explore and see what else might fall into those categories. When these things become routine, the energy once focused on your spouse can shift to your personal needs and desires. Sexual intimacy becomes more about what is in it for you rather than meeting the needs of your partner. As selfishness increases, intimacy decreases.

Keeping It Fresh

One of the greatest ways to keep your love life energized over time is to discuss sex with your spouse during nonintimate times. Be objective and listen actively. Ask open-ended questions that encourage discussion. Instead of asking "Are you happy with our sex life?" ask "From your perspective, what could we do to improve our sex life?" The second question gives permission to voice an opinion that doesn't have to be justified or supported with facts. No matter how good a relationship is, there's always room for improvement. Also, using the words *we* and *our* shows that you are interested in improving as a couple. Contrast this with the question "How could I be a better lover for you?" This may seem like a selfless question, but it puts tremendous pressure on the partner being asked to answer honestly without hurting feelings. Communication leads to understanding, which is a starting point to improving intimacy.

The next step in overcoming monotony is making intentional choices to add variety to your relationship. Albert Einstein said, "The definition of insanity is doing the same thing over and over again and expecting different results." This is as true in the bedroom as it is in any other aspect of life.

Imagine you've fallen into the habit of making love every Saturday morning. You wake up in the same bed at the same time. You initiate sex in the customary manner. Your partner responds exactly as you expect them to, and so on and so forth. This goes on for months, maybe even years. It's just what you do. How do you spell boredom? R-o-u-t-i-n-e. There's nothing inherently wrong with this scenario. It can be both comfortable and satisfying. Just don't let routine encounters be your only sexual encounters. Choose a different day of the week, time of day, or room of the house.

A few times a year, Tara and I will go somewhere overnight without the kids. It is always time well spent. Intimacy in a new venue can change everything. Once our long-standing patterns are interrupted, we find ourselves reinventing the entire process. After thirty-plus years of marriage, we continue to discover new experiences that we both find incredible, but it requires taking time to step outside our normal routine.

Rule of Engagement: We will make efforts to keep sex fresh and fight routine and boredom.

Discussion Questions

- On a scale of one to ten, with one being "I never want to talk about sex" and ten being "I can talk about anything," how comfortable are you in terms of discussing sex with your spouse? What could help you to be more comfortable?

- Individually, list the top three sexual experiences that you have had as a married couple. Come together and discuss your lists. How similar or different are your lists? What specifically makes them different? How does this translate into what each of you most desire from sex?

- How aligned are you in terms of frequency and patterns for your sex life? Does one of you have greater control over your sex life, or is it shared equally?

- Would you say you are more spontaneous or routine in your sex life? Do you desire more spontaneity or more routine? Why?

- Plan a special night for sex. It might be at a hotel or just at home, but make it a point to vary this from your typical encounter. Think about your answers from the earlier question: what could you do to make this night a top three experience from your spouse's perspective?

Outside Influences

I have some friends who have recently married. For both of them, it is a second marriage. He brings three children into the mix, and she brings two. They are the picture of a blended family. Like any newlywed couple, they have both their joys and their struggles. They are learning day by day and week by week what it means to be in a committed relationship. I asked them recently to define their biggest marriage challenge. They were unified in their response. It's the outside influences they deal with on a daily basis. Both members of this couple have to deal with an ex who shares custody of their children. To further complicate things, both of their exes have remarried, bringing another voice and opinion into their world. "If marriage were just about us, it would be easy," they say. "It's all the other people that interfere that make it tough."

Marriage is the beginning of a new nuclear family, which is why Genesis 2:24 says, "A man leaves his father and mother and is united to his wife, and they become one flesh." This verse is where the phrase "leave and cleave" originates. Marriage might be easier if it was only the two of you, but unless you live on a deserted island, in-laws, coworkers, friends, exes, children, and others will have some level of influence in and on your relationship. Not all influences are bad. You are probably aware of many godly marriages that you could learn from and model. However, no other relationship is exactly like yours.

Creating the New Nuclear Family

The first significant external influence that most couples face are former nuclear families and in-laws. You may know on an intellectual level that your spouse is your "new" family, but living that out can be challenging. The passage in Genesis says, "They become one flesh," which implies a process over time. Sexual intimacy is a key part of this oneness, but becoming one also happens over time as the couple begins to share life together. Common thoughts, dreams, and goals are all included in this concept. After thirty-five years of marriage, Tara can finish most of my sentences. It's hard to surprise her because she can almost always figure out what I'm planning before I make it known. But this certainly doesn't happen overnight. So it is important to protect your relationship in the early years until this one flesh mind-set becomes natural and intuitive.

Before you can become a new nuclear family, you have to extricate yourself from your old one. While this is more applicable to a young person marrying, it still holds true to some degree as you age. As a married couple, you have to intentionally break the old bond that existed with your parents. That doesn't mean abandon, but it does mean establishing and communicating that a new relationship is now being formed. While ideally parents would understand this and "let go," that is not always the case.

As a father of two adult married sons I know that it can be hard as a parent to let go. It's a strange phenomenon. One day I'm Dad providing guidance and counsel, and the next day, my son is married, and my job has suddenly changed. I see him being strongly influenced by his wife and making decisions differently than I would have suggested. But it's no longer my place to direct. I'm still here to offer advice when asked, but I have to recognize that he is leading his own family now. As hard as this was with my sons, I can't imagine what it will be like when my daughter goes from under my wing to the wing of her future husband. But I know even now that I will have to honor that new relationship.

A husband has to learn to depend on his wife and prioritize her needs and desires over those of his parents, especially his mother.

This can be an early and ongoing point of contention in marriage, especially if wife and mother begin competing for his attention and his favor. Many men don't even see this happening, but I can guarantee you that their wives do.

My parents would come to visit us when we lived out of state, typically for several days at a time. My mom was the type who wanted to help everyone when she could, and she certainly wasn't one to sit idle. During one of their visits, Tara and I were both away at work while mom was at our house. She noticed a small stain in the grout of our white tiled kitchen floor. She found some kind of scouring powder and an old toothbrush and began to clean. The next thing you know, she had spent the entire afternoon on her hands and knees cleaning all of the grout in our kitchen.

Since they were in town, I managed to come home from work early. After greeting me with a hug, she told me that she was really tired and informed me of what she had done. While it was not something I would have noticed, I sincerely appreciated the effort. An hour later, Tara arrived home from work. I immediately told her what Mom had done, thinking that she would be thrilled. To my surprise, Tara looked perturbed, but she graciously thanked Mom anyway. What I perceived as my Mom being helpful, Tara saw as condemnation of her housekeeping. Whether Mom meant it that way or not, I'll never know. But I'll never convince Tara that it was not a veiled criticism.

Over time, I learned that one way I could support my wife was to redirect my mom when she started "helping." I either convinced my mom to do something else, or I would step in and say, "Let me do that." Even if that didn't always work, Tara appreciated my awareness and support.

Wives are not exempt from family ties either. If a woman has had a strong father in her life, it can be very tough for her to suddenly put total trust into a new man, even when that man is her husband. In many cases, a woman may come from a situation where Daddy has provided for her every need and whim. There weren't many things she had to do without. Now that she's married, the couple may be taking several steps backward from a financial standpoint, and she may be forced to live within a budget for the first time in her life. How difficult must it be for her to deny a desire when she knows that she could fulfill it with a simple request to her father? Perhaps it's not a financial tie that controls her. In other situations, wives have come from a domineering father to whom she could never say no. Suddenly, the desires of the husband may directly conflict with the desires of the father. She may be faced with saying no to her father for the first time in her life.

I remember in our early years of marriage, we would travel back home for holidays. Staying at my parent's home was always comfortable (at least for me), but I hated staying with Tara's parents. It wasn't just her parents at issue; it was also Tara herself. She became a different person when she returned to their home. Her attitude changed, her demeanor, even her vocabulary. Essentially, she reverted back to the person that she was when she was living at their home under her parent's authority. I would hear her agree to things that I knew she opposed and silence her opinion on issues that she felt strongly about. It drove me crazy. I would wonder who abducted my wife and replaced her with this person?

Tara would say that the reverse happened when we would stay at my parent's house. I would become a "helpless little boy" who allowed my mother to wait on me hand and foot. In hindsight, Tara's commands for me "get up and get it yourself" should have been a clue to her frustration! As it turns out, each of us reverted back to the person and role that we had played when we were living with our parents. It's hard to establish a new nuclear family if we don't begin to perform in our new roles. This duality is unhealthy in any setting, and it led to a rule that we both eventually agreed to.

Rule of Engagement: Don't let the people around us dictate who we are.

You aren't always blessed with in-laws who want the best for you as a couple. I can think of several marriages that were wrecked by underhanded parents. In each case, the parents felt from the beginning that the chosen spouse was not good enough for their child.

Through a variety of devious means, these parents manipulated and sabotaged the marriage and then made themselves out to be heroes as they swooped in to rescue the abandoned child. If you find yourself in a situation like this, for the good of your marriage, run! Marriage is hard without having someone on the outside working to separate you. There may come a time when you can reestablish that relationship with appropriate boundaries, but until then, prioritize your spouse and your one-flesh union.

Keeping Children in Perspective

The presence of children can and will influence your marriage. From birth, your kids will want and demand your individual attention and show clear signs of jealousy when they see your attention diverted to your spouse. While this is very natural, it should not be catered to. God has given us a specific order regarding our relationships. Our first priority is to be to God Himself, our second is to our spouse (the person with whom we've become one with), and our third is to our children.

I see many couples that are so worn out from meeting the needs of their kids that they have no energy left for their marriage. They take the time to drive their kids to a seemingly endless list of activities but can't seem to schedule the occasional date night. I've heard many husbands bemoan the fact that their wives will do virtually anything for the kids, but when it comes time to attending to their physical needs, they are met with the "I'm too exhausted" routine. Over time, this will create an unhealthy sense of jealousy and resentment that has no place in a godly marriage.

Rule of Engagement: Keep your spouse a top priority.

Keeping your spouse a top priority begins with intentionally spending time together without your children. Start when the kids are young. Find a reliable baby sitter and take the occasional evening out for date night. So many couples I know have kids who are entering school age but have never left their kids with a sitter. It's not about spending more time with your spouse than with your kids, but merely spending intentional time with the person you have committed to in marriage. At some point, the kids leave home, and it's important to still have a solid relationship with the person who stays behind with you.

Rule of Engagement: Agree on parenting style early and often.

I had a lifelong friend who got married in his late thirties. It seemed that he was the exact opposite of his new bride. From a social and political perspective, he was extremely conservative. She, on the other hand, was very liberal in her worldviews. And yet they were a neat couple. They would get into some crazy arguments over various things, but they kept their differences in perspective. Within three years of getting married, they had two lovely little girls. As the babies became toddlers, they discovered the need for some type of discipline. And that's when the conflict began. My buddy was of the firm opinion that a swat on the behind was the most effective form of training. His wife was absolutely appalled at any form of physical discipline. Her approach was one of putting the girls in time-out and then discussing their behavior to help them realize the error in their ways. This was the first time in their marriage that their differences in approach and opinion affected lives beyond their own. Without having agreed on a philosophy and discipline technique, they found themselves in a heated debate, in front of the girls, every time a correction was required.

One Saturday, this family and another family with similarly aged kids were at our home for a social gathering. All six kids were in the basement with us dads, while the moms were all upstairs preparing dinner. Everyone was having a good time when our other friend's little girl suddenly began crying and ran to her dad. "Suzie bit me!" she screamed as she pointed directly at my conservative friend's daughter. He immediately grabbed his daughter Suzie, turned her to face him, and asked her "Did you bite Sally?" "Yes," she calmly replied. This was not the answer he was hoping for. Had she denied it, he could have given her an idle threat to behave and moved on.

So, not sure what else to do, he repeated his question, "I asked you, did you bite Sally?" And once again, she calmly replied, "Yes." I knew that he wanted to give her a little spanking as a consequence for her behavior, but he knew the degree to which this would upset his wife. Not knowing what else to do, he finally sternly told her not to do it again. He later shared with me how disempowered this made him feel. In spite of all of the differences they had learned to manage, this was one area that really caused our friends friction in their marriage.

Rule of Engagement: We will be unified in our parenting approach.

It's important to discuss and agree upon parenting issues before you are directly confronted with them. When the kids are young, what types of discipline are acceptable to use and under what circumstances? As the kids get older, what is your policy on visiting friends or sleepovers? In the teen years, what is the minimum age for dating? What is the curfew? Gaining alignment with your spouse on these areas is critical, and it is much easier to achieve when you're not under the pressure of making a specific decision that has not been discussed.

Having agreed upon and communicated rules will keep your kids from going to the "easy" parent to get what they want. Kids learn early on which parent to ask for each situation. Often, parents feed this type of behavior with statements like, "Okay, but don't tell your mother" or "We'll buy this thing, but your father doesn't need to know." This teaches your children that their parents are not unified. But it also teaches them that they can play one parent against the other to serve their own advantage. I learned to never consent to my children's requests without first asking them, "Have you asked your mother? What did she say?" If I learned that Tara had already said no, I would not contradict her. If they hadn't asked her, I would either make a decision on the spot or tell them I needed to discuss the request with her first. By having discussions with your spouse during a time of no pressure, you will learn the appropriate approach for each situation.

Rule of Engagement: We will not let our kids play us against each other.

I was very close with my mom, especially during my teen years, and would go to her to vent on days whenever I had hit my limit of frustration with my dad. Being raised on a farm, I found myself working for and with my dad throughout my youth. While he was a great man, he was hard to please and had high expectations for the work that I did for him. There were times when it felt like no matter how hard I tried, I couldn't satisfy him. During those times, more than anything else, I wanted Mom to take my side and stand up to Dad on my behalf. She would listen. She would advise. But she would never side with me against Dad. She would remind me that he was her husband, and they were a unified front. While she was sorry that I was angry, I'd have to either move past it or work my issues out directly with him. Little did I know how much I would come to appreciate her example when raising teen boys of my own!

There may be legitimate times when you and your spouse don't agree on an issue, or the situation may require more discussion. We've had many situations where one of us has told our kids no and the other did not understood why. When we discuss the specifics, away from the children, sometimes we will come to see the other's reasoning for denial, and other times we will collectively agree that it would be okay to change our answer to "yes" instead. If we decide something should change, the original decision maker is the one to go back and give the revised answer. Allowing the original parent the opportunity to communicate sends the message that sometimes answers change, once due consideration has been given or as more information has become available.

Representing Our Spouse to Others

Our words can either enhance our relationships or tear them down. We need to think carefully not only about what we say *to* our spouses but also what we say *about* them to others.

Kind words are like honey – sweet to the soul and healthy for the body. (Proverbs 16:24, NLT)

[T]he tongue is a small thing that makes grand speeches. But a tiny spark can set a great forest of fire. And among all the parts of the body, the tongue is a flame of fire. It is a whole world of wickedness corrupting your entire body. It can set your whole life on fire, for it is set on fire by hell itself. (James 3:5–6, NLT)

I remember as a kid I had an uncle who delighted in telling stories about his wife at holiday dinners. While they were intended to be humorous, they typically involved some mistake or misstep my aunt had made since our last gathering. As he would begin each story, she would plead with him not to share it, which just seemed to increase his eagerness to tell the tale. Even though I was a young man at the time, I recall the discomfort I felt watching my aunt blush and attempt to hide her embarrassment.

My uncle was not alone in this behavior. I've seen many people use their spouse as fodder for humorous stories. I've heard many women emasculate their husbands when they publicly ridicule their inability to repair things or get things done around the house. Sadly, these conversations often become a bit of a competition within the group. It's not uncommon after hearing one such story to hear another person try to top the first one, "You think that's bad? My wife is so dumb that she…" And so it goes, with each person trying to outdo the spouse described before. Over time, when we speak of our spouse in a demeaning manner, we begin to believe our own words. Even when meant as humor, our disrespect begins to build. The line between humor and resentment can be very thin.

Avoid Toxic Influences

While we should think carefully about how we represent our spouse to others, we must also guard our hearts against what we allow others to say to us about our spouse. I know of several relationships that ended in divorce when one of the partners became immersed in a negative social environment. One friend of mine had been married for about ten years and had two young daughters. I remember his excitement when his wife took a new job at a local company. With her significant increase in pay, he was very excited about what their future would hold. But within six months of starting her job, she filed for divorce.

It turns out that in her new position, she found herself in a department filled with divorced women that had all developed bitterness toward marriage and men in general. In her early time there, she would tell "funny" stories about something her husband had done, mostly in an effort to break the ice and forge relationships. But before long, she began to get unsolicited feedback and advice from her peers. "You deserve better," "I wouldn't put up with that," even "I left my husband when he did that." Though it wasn't her original intent, her desire to fit in opened the door for unwanted opinions. Eventually, their words chipped away at the foundation of her marriage until the foundation was completely destroyed. You may have heard the old saying "Hurt people, hurt people." If you are not lifting your marriage up to serve as a light for others, you run the risk of having their darkness bring you down. We can't always control who surrounds us, but we can control what we say and believe. We need to make the protection of our marriage the highest priority. That means not tearing it down (even in humor) around others. And it means building up our spouse at every opportunity both directly and to others.

Positive Outside Influences

While avoiding toxic influences is wise, we should all seek out positive relationships that can help us grow our marriages in a God-honoring manner.

Tara and I led a life group through our church, with six or seven couples that regularly attended. The group became very close in terms of sharing and building relationships. One week, someone invited a friend to attend our group. We didn't know very much about this lady other than she was separated from her husband and raising a son from a prior marriage on her own.

She began to attend each week and over time began to open up to the group. One week during prayer time, she told us that she and her estranged husband had decided to file for divorce. Having been through this once before, she expressed the pain and hassle associated with the process. She asked us as a group if we could pray for her divorce, specifically that it would go as smoothly and efficiently as possible.

In that moment, the Spirit moved within our group, which led me to reply, "I'm sorry. We will not pray for your divorce. However, we will pray for your reconciliation and for your future as a family." There was stunned silence across the group, yet everyone knew this was what we were called to do. Her response was one of defiance, "I think we're way past that. I would just appreciate if you would all just pray that we get through this as simply as possible."

At that moment, another member of the group asked if he could invite her husband to the following week's gathering. She replied that she didn't care but didn't think he would ever consider attending. The following week, he surprised us all by showing up. He had an attitude, but he was there. I'll never forget how he sat in a chair, removed from the group, with his arms crossed defiantly across his chest. We held our study as normal then went into prayer time. His request was identical to hers from the week before, and our response to him was the same, "Sorry. We're just not going to pray for that."

This continued on for several weeks, with both of them in attendance but sitting on opposite sides of the room. Each week we would pray fervently for their reconciliation. In time, we began to sense a softening between them. A few weeks later and they began to sit beside each other. Fast forward a couple months and our life group spent a Saturday moving all of his possessions back into their home! God completely restored their marriage and went on to equip them to become leaders in the church. That was almost fifteen years ago. Now this couple has grandchildren, and they live an incredibly blessed life. And it's all because a group of people felt led to pray for their marriage instead of against it. With prayer, they were able to change their vision from one of separation and divorce to one of living together in a strong rebuilt marriage. Their foundation is firmly built on rock today, and they have become an inspiration to many other couples that are struggling.

Discussion Questions

- Who are the people that have the biggest influence on your marriage? What influence is positive? Negative?

- What specific challenges do you have with your in-laws? What guidelines could you put in place as a couple to minimize these issues?

- Are there are any areas of parenting where you need to align your views? What issues would you like to be unified in as your children get older?

- What can you do to show your children that your marriage is a priority?

- Think of some specific examples where your kids tried to use you against your spouse. How did you handle that? How should you have handled that?

- Imagine you are with a group of your (same sex) friends. They begin belittling their spouses in a humorous manner. What is something you could do or say that would prevent you from joining in?

9

Modeling Your Marriage

Guess what? They're watching! Who's watching? you might ask. It turns out that everyone is watching. Your marriage is in public display for your kids, your families, your friends, your coworkers, and your neighbors. Some of those audiences may care more about what they see than others, but don't think for a minute that people aren't noticing how you and your spouse interact.

People are not just observing your relationship; they are judging it as well. It may not even be intentional, but couples compare their marriage to other marriages all the time. They watch and take note of how you show love, communicate, make decisions, disagree, even raise your kids. In some instances, comparisons can help a couple to feel better about their own marriage. "Well, at least we don't fight like the Watsons." When people see and evaluate a shocking marriage, their takeaway should be different. While they may still see flawed humans, they also see a relationship that they would like to model.

Marriage is a Powerful Testimony of Your Faith

Your marriage can be a powerful witness to those who are not believers. One of the realities of being a Christian is that our unbelieving family and friends are watching to see if our commitment to follow

Jesus affects how we live. If they perceive that our lives are no different from theirs, it may help justify their choice of unbelief.

Many people get married in a church and recite traditional vows. Even if they wed outside of the church, most will still use a minister of some sort. But that is where the similarity between the marriages of believers and nonbelievers ends. Whereas for some, their vows are just "beautiful words," as Christians we are making a covenant vow before God that we will honor, cherish, love, and support our spouse "until death do us part." Christian marriages should be shocking because we are determined to live this out over the course of our lives and our marriages. When the world sees marital discord or divorce in the Christian community, it puts us on an equal playing field. And that's not where we're called to be. We should have marriages that are visibly different from those that don't have Jesus Christ in their lives. Our marriages should be a living testimony of the power of the Holy Spirit, who changes us individually and as a couple. This is evidenced through our sacrificial love and humility, when we admit our wrongs and ask for forgiveness, and when we have joy in the midst of sorrow. People who don't know Jesus should look at us and think, "I want what they've got." And when they ask us why our marriages are different, we should be prepared with an answer (1 Peter 3:15).

Using your marriage as a Christian witness is not about sugarcoating your lives and making sure that you look happy all of the time. It's about being genuine and letting the love of God shine through you. When Tara and I have done our marriage workshops, we solicit feedback from our participants at the end. The most common theme we've heard is how much couples enjoyed our transparency and our authenticity. This always struck me as odd because to us that is our normal way of living. When we're with friends or in a small group setting, we strive to be genuine with what is going on in our lives. Why is that so rare? So many Christian couples put on a façade that everything in their world is nearly perfect. The reality is none of us lives a sinless life, and nobody has a perfect marriage. Yet when around church friends, that is often how we portray our lives.

As an elder at our church, it would grieve me when I would learn that a couple in our congregation was seeking a divorce. Usually, by the time I would have a chance to talk with them, they had made up their minds, and it was too late to salvage the relationship. When I would talk with their friends or their small group leaders to see if they had seen this coming, I would hear that they were as surprised as I was to hear the news. People living life with the couple were unaware of the problems that lurked behind closed doors. I wonder how many times these couples would argue all the way to church or to their small group meeting, only to put on a smile once they arrived, indicating they had no need for prayer or counsel. This is not how we are called to live. Imagine if couples embraced the freedom they have as believers and opened up to the people who were closest to them. Perhaps they could have received help before issues got out of hand. Every relationship has problems. We need to develop Christian community with trusted friends who can guide us through the rough patches and confirm that we are not alone.

Lessons from Our Youth

My parents were my first marriage role models. My father was a tremendous husband for the entire seventy-three years of his marriage. I never doubted that my dad loved my mom because he demonstrated his love in ways I could easily see. Every year in June a single rose would appear in a bud vase. This was not to celebrate their wedding anniversary, but the anniversary of their first date. Not a year went by without seeing that rose on the table. My mom would practically glow every time it would appear. When my mom passed away a couple of years ago, Dad had seventy-three roses placed on her casket as a tribute to their incredible marriage.

We lived in a farmhouse with a detached, unheated garage. My mom taught school in a neighboring town and had to leave for work quite early in the mornings, often in the dark and cold of winter. Dad would go outside, shovel snow, get to the car, and have it running and warm before she needed to leave. Mom never climbed into an icy car and never had to walk through snow to leave for work.

Dad was a constant flirt. I distinctly remember Mom standing at the stove cooking dinner. He couldn't walk by without "goosing" her. She would feign shock and disgust, but I would always notice the resulting smile from the attention he had paid her.

My father was not the perfect husband. I'm sure there were times when my mom was frustrated or aggravated with something he had done. But honestly, I don't remember those instances. What I do remember is what he imprinted on my mind: a wife is a person to hold in the highest regards and to love and respect above anyone else.

Mom always told people that one of her greatest charges in life was to raise four great future husbands. From an early age, she taught us how to cook and clean and always be respectful of women. She warned us that if we left our clothes on the floor, our future wives would be very frustrated. There is no doubt in my mind that this pattern of modeling and intentional teaching is the reason that my brothers and I are all in such great marriages.

You may have come from a broken or dysfunctional home. Or you may have been the product of a loving but single parent. The behaviors you saw modeled may not be anything that you want to replicate. You don't have to fall into the patterns you were raised with. You can model your marriage after other couples, or even after the teachings of Jesus. Showing unconditional love, freely showing grace and forgiveness, using kind and encouraging words are all ways that you can build a shocking marriage for yourselves.

Modeling Marriage for Your Kids

"Every father should remember that one day his son will follow his example instead of his advice" (Charles F Kettering). It's important that you choose to create a positive model for your kids. No one will be more impacted by your marriage than the young people watching it every day. You might be able to hide some of your issues from your friends and neighbors, but your kids see you in all situations. They will see your marriage for what it is, warts-and-all. Having a marriage built on a solid foundation can provide your children with tremendous security. A shocking marriage is one of the greatest gifts you can give them.

We should not hide the hard parts of marriage from our kids. Pretending that there are never disagreements is not honest, and it deprives them of the opportunity to learn from watching an effective conflict gain resolution. If you have implemented rules of engagement for conflict, you don't need to be afraid of arguing in front of your children. You'll not be shouting, name-calling, or belittling your spouse. While your arguments may be intense at times, your children will see how you ultimately get to resolution and realize that marriage can be a safe place to disagree. While it may not be your direct intent, this type of positive modeling will teach them how to effectively deal with conflict in their own lives.

Watching how you cope with tough times is another opportunity for learning. Whether you're grieving the loss of a loved one or in a season of financial uncertainty, kids who see their parents rely on each other and on God will gain a sense of peace and security. Letting your kids see that you are human and struggle on occasion is not a bad thing. In fact, allowing them to see you dealing with such struggles in a positive manner is invaluable. It's okay if children walk in and find their parents arguing. But it's fantastic if they walk in and see their parents praying together. Don't underestimate the power of their observation and the long-term impact it will have on their lives.

Helping your children understand the unique relationship that you have with your spouse is of critical importance. I am the father of three sons and have been (or am going through) the teen years with each of them. Testosterone-filled boys will naturally become aggressive and assert themselves in an attempt to establish their boundaries and to understand their true role in the family. This can lead to outbursts, arguments, raised voices and even veiled threats. I distinctly remember a time when my oldest son got into an argument with his mother. It started out like most arguments, but began to increase in terms of its intensity. I stood nearby watching to see where this was headed. At one point he got so angry that he took both of his hands and physically pushed her. At that point I grabbed him by his shirt, pulled him away and got right in his face. "That is my wife!" I said sternly. "I will not allow you or any other man to get physical with her or disrespect her like that." At that moment, I was no longer just

Dad. I was Mom's husband, and was protecting her as such. Truth be told, that was such an effective technique that I used it for each of his younger brothers when the appropriate situations arose. Years later, my two older sons each told me what an impactful moment that was for them, and it gave them a powerful lesson on how to respect their own wives.

Another important thing we can model for our children is the way we show physical affection to our spouse. Too often, we're more willing to argue than to kiss in front of our children. God forbid they realize we're in love. Physical affection, like all other areas in our marriage, is one where we are modeling behaviors that our kids will one day mimic.

Think about it, our culture bombards us with sexual messages in every area except for marriage. While young singles in movies and television are always on the prowl for sex, married couples are often depicted as bored, frustrated, or oblivious. Even today, young adults feel their parents only had sex to procreate. With the exception of "the talk" where we explain the mechanics of making babies, we don't talk about sex as an expression of love, with our kids. We don't flirt with our spouses in front of them. What is the message being drilled into their heads? Get plenty while you're single because there's no sex after marriage.

As a couple, we've always been very open about sex around our kids. Not in a graphic or exhibitionist manner, but our children know that we are sexually active within our marriage. Our older married sons seem to now respect and appreciate that we were open about that part of our relationship. But as you would imagine, it still makes our teens quite uncomfortable.

The importance of letting children see the sexual chemistry between their parents is one of the most surprising things that couples hear from us during our workshops. It's not something most of them experienced growing up, so it's not something they've considered sharing with their own children. Most of them understand the logical reasoning, but many struggle with actually showing affection. Once we remind them that their children are seeing passion in almost every other setting, they typically agree as to its importance.

Rule of Engagement: We will strive to be transparent with our marriage in front of our children so that they can see a shocking marriage modeled for their own lives.

If you don't think modeling is effective, let me give you a brief example. A few years ago, I came home from work, set my stuff on the table, and walked behind my wife as she was working at the stove. Without thinking twice, I patted her on the bottom and said, "Hey, babe." (my usual greeting upon arriving home). But this particular time, she unexpectedly turned to me and said, "That's where he got it!" Then she burst out laughing. Unbeknownst to me, she had gotten a call from school that day. Our then-eight-year-old son had walked behind his teacher while she was writing on the board and done the same thing to her. The school was appalled. In an odd way, I was quite proud.

Mentor and Be Mentored

Christian discipleship is the process of having believers who are more mature in the faith work with those who are newer in the faith to become more like Jesus over time. Many churches offer training in this area or have whole programs dedicated to this idea. Scripture shows us that the apostle Paul had a relationship with Timothy, a younger believer whom he mentored. At the same time, he had a relationship with Barnabas, a believer more mature in his faith. No matter where we are in our walk, I think we are called to have the same type of relationships. Someone further along than we are who can help us as we enter new situations, and someone newer in the faith that we ourselves can guide.

While this is a proven model for Christian living, I think it can be expanded to include a focus on marriage. Imagine if every couple had a trusted mentor-couple whom they could be completely transparent with—a relationship with no judgment or condemnation. An environment where any question could be asked and answered with no embarrassment. Where topics could range from sex to finance to relations with in-laws.

In many ways we keep our marriages so private that every couple is forced to recreate the proverbial wheel. Seeking out a mentor-couple could save considerable time and emotional energy. Don't know what to do when your two-year old is throwing a tantrum? You want to discipline, but your husband wants to ignore. There are couples that have been through that and can offer guidance. Feeling like your sex life is in a state of rapid decline? You're not the first to experience it. There are couples that have worked through the same experience and are better off for it.

Rule of Engagement: We will be open to learning behaviors and practices from other couples that will benefit us in our own marriage.

But as you are mentored, you should consider finding a younger couple that can benefit from your marriage experience. Finding an older couple that can help you through life is wonderful. Finding a younger couple that you can help is fantastic too.

Modeling the Gospel for a Watching World

God didn't intend for His design of marriage to be shocking. He intended for it to be the standard. But a marriage that reflects His will stands out in our fallen world.

Marriage is a covenant relationship that reflects Christ's love for the church. Ephesians 5:25 says, "Husbands, love your wives, just as Christ loved the church, and gave himself up for her." We should model this type of sacrificial love in our marriages. Our first love must be God, but our second love must be for our spouse. Only then can we truly model the gospel to a watching world.

Discussion Questions

- What kind of role model for marriage did you have growing up? How does this compare/contrast with your spouse? What behaviors that you saw do you want to incorporate into your marriage? What behaviors do you want to avoid?

- What kind of model are you providing to your kids? What would their takeaway be if they saw you in an argument? What if they saw you kissing?

- Can you think of an older couple that has a shocking marriage? Are there things you can learn from watching them?

- What does your marriage say to a watching world? Do they see the gospel being modeled through your relationship? How could you put more emphasis on this?

- If Christ loved the Church and gave himself up for her, what does it look like give yourself up for your spouse?

10

Effective Communication

A good man brings good things out of the good
stored up in his heart, and an evil man brings
evil things out of the evil stored up in his heart.
For the mouth speaks what the heart is full of.

—Luke 6:45

Effective communication is the last chapter of this book, for a reason. Certainly not because it's the least important. Quite the contrary. Lack of communication seems to be one of the primary concerns that couples in distress complain about in their relationships. Effective communication consists of multiple, distinct parts, what is said, how it is said, and how it is received.

The Power of Your Words

We've discussed throughout this book how to enhance various aspects of your marriage. Hopefully by now your heart is full of love and respect for your spouse. When that is the case, the words that you speak will reflect those feelings. You should never have to search for "something nice to say." Such sentiments will come naturally when your heart is right. Conversely, before you speak out critically against your spouse, you should first look to your own heart to understand your motivations. If you are struggling with this, take it to the Lord in prayer. Use the power of the Holy Spirit to soften or even change your heart.

Rule of Engagement: I will search my heart before I say something unkind.

This can be a tough rule to follow, especially after a bad day or in the heat of conflict. But it is critical to understand how destructive our words can be. Consider the following passage in James 3:3–12:

> When we put bits into the mouths of horses to make them obey us, we can turn the whole animal. Or take ships as an example. Although they are so large and are driven by strong winds, they are steered by a very small rudder wherever the pilot wants to go. Likewise, the tongue is a small part of the body, but it makes great boasts. Consider what a great forest is set on fire by a small spark. The tongue also is a fire, a world of evil among the parts of the body. It corrupts the whole body, sets the whole course of one's life on fire, and is itself set on fire by hell. All kinds of animals, birds, reptiles and sea creatures are being tamed and have been tamed by mankind, but no human being can tame the tongue. It is a restless evil, full of deadly poison. With the tongue we praise our Lord and Father, and with it we curse human beings, who have been made in God's likeness. Out of the same mouth come praise and cursing. My brothers and sisters, this should not be. Can both fresh water and salt water flow from the same spring? My brothers and sisters, can a fig tree bear olives, or a grapevine bear figs? Neither can a salt spring produce fresh water.

Obviously, this is not a new challenge that is unique to our culture. Since the fall of man, our words have had the power to tear one another down. It's great, and important, to apologize if we stumble and use words we regret. It is so much better to avoid saying harsh words to begin with. While forgiveness should occur, words cannot be unheard.

Expectations of Communication

I'll never forget the first time I led a marriage study. I was the leader of a church small group that consisted of eight couples ranging in age from their thirties to their fifties. Each group was allowed to choose the topic of the study they wanted to pursue, be it a book of the Bible or a relevant topical study. Our group decided they wanted to do a study on making marriages stronger. At the time, I didn't consider myself an expert in this area, but I figured I, with Tara's help, could facilitate a discussion on this topic as well as any other we had done. I went to the Christian Bookstore and selected a book, purchased study guides for everyone, and began the study the following week. We were in our fourth session when we hit the lesson on communication. While we normally just covered the discussion questions as a group, on this particular evening, I kept the men in one room, and Tara took the women in another. We asked each group to identify the biggest issues that they faced in terms of communication within their marriage. The men were done in fifteen minutes and relocated to the food table. After about forty-five minutes, the women finished their discussion, and we brought the groups back together to share the lists.

For the most part, the husbands did not see lack of communication as a problem. When urged to come up with something, they listed that they wanted their wives to communicate more clearly, more specifically, and at more appropriate times (e.g., not in the middle of a televised football game).

The women had a much more extensive list, including their desire for more-frequent higher-quality communication. They wanted their husbands to be better listeners and be more willing to share their feelings. None of this was a surprise to the husbands; most had heard these requests before. Then the women shared a final item that left the men speechless. "We expect you to know what we want or need without us having to tell you." After a long and awkward silence, one of the husbands began to laugh nervously, which caused all the other men in the group to join in. They thought the wives were striving to be humorous with such an outrageous request. After a few minutes of laughter and sarcastic commentary, the men looked up to notice that the women were not laughing; in fact, they weren't even smiling. The wives saw no humor in this, as they had meant their comment quite literally. The biggest shock for me was that my wife was right there with them, looking just as offended as the other ladies!

The conversation became quite animated. The women would not back down. The men saw this request as absurd. Here I was trying to lead a marriage enrichment study, and couples were headed home barely speaking to one another.

After that evening, Tara and I had our own conversation about this controversial request. While she agreed with the point the women were making, she could also appreciate how that put men in a no-win situation. We decided that being attentive could allow a spouse to anticipate preferences and moods, but no one should be held accountable for being a mind reader. Effective communication starts with vocalization, not telepathy. This became our first rule of engagement outside of conflict.

Rule of Engagement: I will not expect my spouse to know my wants and needs if I don't communicate them.

This rule eliminated much of the frustration and anger under the surface just waiting to erupt. If Tara was having a tough day, when I arrived home, she would tell me, "I need a break. Do something with the kids." Upon hearing that, I was happy to jump in and honor her request. Hearing her need allowed me to reprioritize my mental to-do list and not just jump into a task that I had been planning without considering her needs. This provided her with the break she deserved but also kept her from resenting me because I didn't offer her assistance without being asked.

As marriages mature, couples become more in tune with their partner's needs. It's a beautiful thing when someone can anticipate and satisfy their spouse's desires without being asked. But don't let resentment set in if you don't ask, and they don't respond.

When Communication Isn't...

I still remember my freshman communications class in college. The bulk of the class taught students how to make a variety of presentations and speeches. But there was one early lecture that focused on the theory of communication. The professor provided a diagram showing that there was always a source of communication and there was a target. There have always been a variety of ways that the message can be transmitted, but there is always a sender and a receiver. Sometimes there is a barrier between the two that can disrupt or distort the communication. Most importantly, a message sent but not received is not communication.

During the first session of our marriage workshops, we ask couples to share their top marriage frustrations. While men's answers will vary from man to man and from group to group, women almost always say they want their husbands to communicate more. You can tell from the look on the men's faces that this is not the first time they've heard this, but they are not sure what to do about it.

It's no secret that men and women communicate differently. Women are typically much better multitaskers than men. My mom and my wife shared this interesting skill. They were both able to do dishes, make grocery lists, follow a television show that was on in the kitchen, and listen to a story that I was telling them at the same time. It was not uncommon for me to lose my own train of thought with all the distraction around me. But if I were to ever ask either of them what I'd been saying, they could recall my last ten sentences almost verbatim. That has always been incomprehensible to me.

Men tend to be very focused on one item at a time. I can't tell you how many times I've been surprised to learn that we were meeting some couple for dinner when I was planning on a simple evening at home. As hard as I would try, I could not recall ever hearing of such a plan or agreeing to such a commitment. Even though Tara insisted "I told you," if I was mentally engaged in another activity when Tara came in and said something, it was a message sent but not received. Just as my college professor would say, "That is not communication."

Distinguishing the Importance of the Message

In our marriage, we have learned that communication naturally falls into different degrees of importance ranging from casual to critical. Each of these is treated with a different level of attention and interaction. In the most casual conversations, we might both find ourselves focused on something different (typically our smartphones). One or the other of us might stumble across something on Facebook and make an audible comment such as "Huh, that's interesting . . ." If the other hears that and is at a point to listen, they will respond, and a conversation will happen. On the other hand, if the other is deeply engrossed in their own train of thought, the comment goes unacknowledged, and that is okay as well. There are no expectations in this regard, so there are no disappointments.

If communication is of a more important nature, we become more intentional about it. We'll start by making sure we have the other person's attention. "Do you have a minute? I want to talk to you about_____." This is a request, and it gives the other an opportunity to either agree to the conversation at that moment or to politely defer to a later time. Out of respect, we will usually make every effort right then to engage, but sometimes we are in the middle of something and will not be able to devote the attention that an important conversation deserves at that moment.

However, when one of us expresses a critical need for conversation, the other agrees to drop what they are doing and give the moment their highest priority and undivided attention. This could mean stopping a conversation with the kids or getting off the phone right away. These times are rare, and we reserve them for situations that really demand immediate, focused attention.

You may think that all of this sounds overly rigid and structured. We have not put each of these specific categories into rules of engagement. In fact, prior to this writing, we've never openly discussed that this is what we do. This is really more of an observation of what we do, recognizing what works for us. Our overarching rule is actually quite simple.

Rule of Engagement: We will give effective communication high priority in our marriage.

My examples above merely show what living out that rule looks like in our relationship. There are other communication tips and tricks that we have picked up over the course of our marriage. Some of these naturally developed over time, and others we learned from married couples that we have tremendous respect for and modeled after.

Problem-Solving vs. Listening

An issue that commonly surfaces in marriages is the misunderstanding of the purpose of some conversations. While no gender stereotypes are absolute, they often represent a majority of the population. One of these stereotypes surrounds the area of problem-solving. Most men are wired to solve problems. Women, on the other hand, often like to process their challenges by thinking out loud through conversation. Many a husband has made the mistake of hearing his wife complain about something, only to be shut down when he tries to remedy the situation. His thinking is straightforward and simple, "My wife has expressed an issue that is troubling her. I will come to her rescue and take care of the problem." When she hears his advice, she may become aggravated because she does not recall asking for help. Both partners end up being frustrated.

After this happens a few times, that husband may assume that his wife never wants his help. When a situation arises where she really would like assistance, she finds him "unresponsive." She feels disappointed and unsupported while he is bewildered and feels like he can't do anything right.

I remember in my early years of marriage expressing my hopeless feeling in this situation to an older married friend of mine. I'll never forget his sage advice. "Jerry, when she starts in on this conversation, just ask her one simple question: 'Is this something that you would like me to help fix, or am I just supposed to listen?'" While I understood the logic in this, I thought it sounded terribly insensitive to actually ask.

Sure enough, within a few days, Tara came home from work in a terribly frustrated mood. She was upset at her boss and coworkers for some situation she had faced during the day. A few minutes into the conversation, I formed an opinion of how she could respond to overcome this problem. But before I could interrupt her with my advice, I remembered the words my friend had offered. When she paused to gather her thoughts, I asked her directly, "Is this something you want my help on, or do you just want me to listen?" I was amazed at her reaction. She cocked her head, thought for a moment, and responded with "I just need you to listen. Thanks." And she went right on with her story as if I'd never interrupted her. She wasn't offended at all. In fact, she really appreciated me asking the question. At that point, my mind wandered, and I admittedly began to grunt the occasional *uh-huh* as she spoke. But even that was okay. As it turns out, she was mentally processing her situation as she verbalized it. I gave her that audience, and it satisfied her *more* than if I had given an unsolicited solution.

That simple question has become natural for us. I no longer have to ask her the question each time. There are times when she'll say, "I really need you to step in and help me with this." In those instances, I engage in the conversation, ask a lot of questions, and do my best to alleviate her stress.

Making Time for Conversation

We live busy lives. Jobs, kids, church, and other social obligations consume a huge percentage of our available time. There will be days and sometimes weeks where communication between spouses is limited to "drive by conversations," where you cross paths as one is entering the house while the other is exiting. While these peak periods will occur, the key is not to allow them to become your new norm. If you stop and think about it, you probably schedule every obligation and family event on some type of calendar. You know well in advance the date and time of Junior's dentist appointment or Suzie's piano recital. There's no reason that we can't schedule time for conversation with our spouse. The reason this doesn't happen is that we take this communication for granted, simply assuming that it will happen organically in its own time. Not scheduling it puts it at the lowest priority. When faced with a time crunch, the lowest priority always falls of the schedule.

I know what you're thinking. Scheduling conversation? That sounds terrible. You can probably picture the awkwardness. You and your spouse sit across the table, look at your watches, and say, "We have fifteen minutes to talk, so you start." It doesn't have to be this way. There are other ways to prioritize communication that are far less rigid.

I spoke in an earlier chapter about Martini Mondays. That's a great, intentional practice, but there are other habits you can create. Make it a point to talk for ten minutes when you both get home from work. There's power in the "how was your day?" question, especially when you take time to listen to the answer. Pillow talk (that time between when you go to bed and when you fall asleep) is a great time to reflect on your day. If you both happen to be morning people, a chat each morning over coffee can be invaluable. Find a time that works for both of you and give it priority. You'll find that in a short while, you will come to look forward to that each day.

Discussion Questions

- On a scale from one to ten (ten being the best), how would you rate the communication in your marriage? How does this compare with the score your spouse gives?

- How often do you say things to your spouse that you later regret? What could you do to reduce or eliminate this?

- What is your biggest frustration in terms of communication with your spouse?

- Do you currently have the opportunity to have regular, uninterrupted conversation? If not, is there some way that you could arrange that?

- What rules of engagement could you put in place to improve on communication in your marriage?

Study Guide

Marriage enrichment is a commonly desired study topic for small groups in churches. This section is written as a guide to be used for such groups. Whereas the questions at the end of each chapter were intended for couples to answer together, this section will provide additional questions (of a less personal nature) that can be comfortably discussed as a group.

As a group, you can determine how many sessions you would like to spend covering this book. As an example, if you choose to do a single chapter a week, it would take you ten weeks to cover all of the material. If you would like to complete it sooner than that, you can combine multiple chapters into a given session.

If you wanted to complete the study in six weeks, I would recommend that you combine chapters 1 and 2 (shocking marriage, building a foundation), chapters 6 and 7 (keep the spark alive, intimacy) and chapters 8 and 9 (outside influences and modeling).

Decide on the duration of your study in advance so that you can assign the reading to your group prior to each meeting. That will allow you to use the following group discussion questions at each meeting.

Establish Trust

It is important to stress with your group that you will be studying and discussing topics over the course of this study that may be of a sensitive nature. Ask the group to agree to not share any comments made during your sessions outside of the group. It is critical that people feel *safe* in sharing thoughts and concerns within your group. Remind the group of this multiple times over the course of the study, especially once sensitive information has been shared by someone.

Format

Open each session with prayer. Pray specifically for the couples in your group and ask for God's blessing on each marriage represented there.

Discuss any updates from the prior week's prayer requests.

Encourage couples to share any learning, insights or "aha moments" they may have uncovered during their reading and discussion of the material.

Promote an atmosphere of transparency. Lead by example - share your own answers first. You want couples to be able to share areas in which they may be struggling or in commitments they want to be held accountable to. Ask the couples if anyone wants to share any of the answers they came up with at the end of each chapter.

Once you get to chapter 3, encourage couples to share any rules of engagement they have created within their own marriages. Continue to do this for each subsequent week. You will find that other couples will benefit from this, and it may spur them on to create similar rules for themselves.

Go through the following group questions. Have multiple people answer each question. Encourage discussion and debate. Help the group to go beyond superficial answers to share personal stories or opinions where applicable.

At the end of each session, ask for prayer requests. Ask how the group can hold up each marriage in terms of their specific challenges or struggles.

Assign reading for the next session.

Chapter 1: Shocking Marriage

Questions:

- Describe the fanciest wedding that you ever attended. What stood out about it?

- Describe your own wedding. What were the most memorable elements of it?

- Do you see a connection between the size/cost of a wedding and the long-term happiness of the couple? Why/Why not?

- In your own words, describe what the author means by a shocking marriage. What does a shocking marriage look like? Give specific examples of things you've personally seen.

- Why is having a vision for your marriage important?

- What does a couple have to do to create a shocking marriage?

Chapter 2: Build A Solid Foundation

Questions:

- Read Matthew 7:24–27 aloud.

- Who was Jesus talking to? What did he want his listeners to take away from His message?

- What does it mean to build your marriage on rock and not sand?

- The author shares his story of his early married life that was built on sand, and how over time he came to rebuild it upon rock. What was the turning point that helped him realize his foundation was fragile at best? What made him decide to rebuild on rock?

- Think about your own marriages. Are there elements to the author's story that you can relate to? Share them with the group.

- Describe in your own words God's design for marriage. How well is our culture aligned with this original design? Be specific.

- What are your thoughts on the Holy Spirit's role in marriage? What does this look like?

Chapter 3: Rules of Engagement

Questions:

- The author talks about the importance of being intentional in your marriage. What does this mean? Why is it important?

- What is the purpose of having rules of engagement? How should they be used?

- The author gives examples of biblical rules of engagement. Can you think of any others that are mentioned in scripture?

- What are the differences between situational and proactive rules of engagement? How and when might each be used? Give examples.

- Has anyone created any rules they would like to share with the group?

Chapter 4: Dealing with Conflict

Questions:

- Is conflict really inevitable in a marriage? Why or why not? (Proverbs 15:18)

- What role does pride take in generating conflict? How can it be recognized? How can it be dealt with? (Proverbs 8:13, Proverbs 16:18–19, 1 Corinthians 4:7)

- The author described the difference in "conflict styles" that he and his wife had coming into the marriage. Can anyone relate with that? Please share your story with the group.

- When should you let an issue go, as opposed to raising it up? What does effectively letting it go look like?

- The author told the story of John and Sue and their mis-guided argument. Who can relate to that? Have you ever been in a situation where you weren't sure about what you were arguing? Can you share that with the group?

- Why is keeping a long-term perspective so important when you find yourselves in an argument? How can you ensure you are doing that?

Chapter 5: Weathering Life's Storms

Questions:

- Does everyone face trials? What does the Bible say about that? (James 1:2–4, 1 Peter 1:6–7, 1 Peter 4:12–13, John 16:33)

- How can we prepare for future trials? Does it make sense to do so? (Proverbs 3:5–6, Joshua 1:9, Psalm 34:19)

- Are there rules you could create based on trials you've been through in the past in your marriage?

- What can you do to help other couples that you know are going through storms?

Chapter 6: Keeping the Spark Alive

Questions:

- Describe some of the needs that we have beyond our basic physical needs such as food and shelter. How many of these can we satisfy on our own? Which can our spouse help to satisfy?

- Why are we typically more focused on our partner's needs early on in the relationship? Why does this attention shift back to ourselves over time?

- Discuss the difference between comfort and complacency. Is comfort bad?

- How do things change relationally in a marriage once children come into the picture? How does this change as the kids get older? What are the dangers of becoming a child-first-focused family?

- Why is planning regular time together so important in a marriage?

Chapter 7: Intimacy

Questions:

- What is God's view on intimacy? (Hebrews 13:4, 1 Corinthians 7:1–5, Malachi 2:15, Proverbs 5:18–19)

- What is the "honeymoon phase" of a marriage? Why does it fade over time? What takes its place?

- Why is control such an issue in terms of intimacy in many marriages?

- The author shared a very personal story of he and his wife agreeing to try an experiment for thirty days. Can any of you relate to that story? In what way? Were you surprised at their learnings? Is this an experiment that you would be willing to try with your spouse?

- Have you heard the women are like Crock-Pots, men are like microwave ovens analogy? What is your take on this? What do you think of the author's opinion?

- How should intimacy evolve over time in a shocking marriage?

Chapter 8: Outside Influences

Questions:

Who are the people in your lives that have an influence on your marriage?

- How do others intentionally or unintentionally influence your marriage?

- How does our culture attempt to influence your marriage? Think books, movies, social media, etc. Give both positive and negative examples.

- What are some practical ways to recognize that your marriage is being affected by outside influences? (Proverbs 12:26; Proverbs 27:9).

- What can you do to minimize the impact of negative influences that you are around? (Deuteronomy 13:5; 1 Corinthians 15:33).

- How can you incorporate positive examples or influences into your marriage?

Chapter 9: Modeling Your Marriage

Questions:

- How are your marriages a reflection of your faith to an observing world? (Titus 2861 2:7–8; Matthew 5:13–16; 1 Corinthians 11:1)

- In what ways can you demonstrate a Godly example of marriage to other couples? Be specific.

- What examples did you have from your parents that you want to replicate? want to avoid?

- Why is it important to provide a positive model of marriage to your children? What does that look like? (Proverbs 22:6, 3 John 4)

Chapter 10: Effective Communication

Questions:

- Why is what we say to our spouse so important? (Psalm 19:14, Psalm 37:30, Matthew 12:37, Ephesians 4:29)

- What barriers to effective communication do you face in your marriage?

- What practical steps could you incorporate to improve the quality of communication within your marriage?

- How well do you identify with the gender roles the author described in terms of communication style? Give examples.

- What are some ways that you could make specific time for conversation in your marriage?

About the Author

Jerry McColgin has never been one to follow a traditional path. He was the only engineer in his class who had higher English SAT scores than math. He has been a lifelong student of people and relationships, fascinated by discerning what works and what doesn't. Jerry began his career at a large corporation where he traveled the world and pioneered work in leading large cross-functional and cross-cultural teams. At the peak of his career, he made the decision to walk away and start his own consulting business. In this capacity, Jerry continued studying consumers and used his findings to help large companies develop new products and services. Never one to fall into routine, Jerry is now in the process of transitioning into full-time ministry as the marriage minister at Thrive Christian Church in Westfield, Indiana.

God led Jerry to marry his high school sweetheart thirty-five years ago in what he describes as "the best decision he ever made." Jerry and his wife, Tara, love being married and working with other couples to help them have the type of relationships that God intends for them to have. They have been blessed with four children and three grandchildren.

Jerry has an industrial engineering degree from Purdue University and an executive MBA from Ashland University.

CPSIA information can be obtained
at www.ICGtesting.com
Printed in the USA
LVHW111436301219
642041LV00004BB/671/P